Curio

o

Gloucestershire

SEVERN VALE AND FOREST OF DEAN

By the same authors:
Curiosities of Gloucestershire — The Cotswolds

To Five Sons,
for continual encouragement
and practical assistance

First published in 1997 by S.B. Publications
c/o 19 Grove Road, Seaford, East Sussex BN25 1TP

ISBN 1 85770 124 0

Printed and bound by MFP Design & Print,
Longford Trading Estate, Thomas Street, Stretford, Manchester M32 0JT

Curiosities of Gloucestershire

Severn Vale and Forest of Dean

A County Guide to the Unusual

by
Margaret Caine
and Alan Gorton

S. B. Publications

Pineapple finial, late seventeenth century, Westbury Court.

CONTENTS

Front cover: The Cathedral, Sculpture Trail, Speech House
Title page: Sweep street furniture, Cheltenham
Back page: Wishing-Fish Clock, Cheltenham

The Stellar Chancel Ceiling, Abbey Church of St. Mary, Tewkesbury.

INTRODUCTION

Here quick Severn like a silver eel
Wriggles through pastures green and pale
stubble.
There sending up its quiet coloured
bubble
Of earth, May Hill floats in a flaming sky.
And, marvelling at all, forgetting trouble,
Here — home again — stand I.

The joyful words of Frederick William Harvey returning in 1918 to his home from the trenches and captivity as a member of the Gloucestershire Regiment, remind us that the Severn, at one time spelt Havren, deriving from Sabrina, a river name in Tacitus' *Annals*, dominates the countryside. It is Britain's longest river, its estuary experiences the second highest tide anywhere in the world, with a range of forty-seven feet (14·5m), and the Severn Bore, a unique spectacle of a tidal wave which several times a year explodes at over ten miles per hour up the lower reaches from the Bristol Channel towards Gloucester, may reach a spectacular six feet (two metres) in height.

The Vale was carved in the Ice Age through rock and clay of many eras. To the west is the Forest of Dean, an ancient coalfield, created by the pre-historic forest here 300 million years ago.

In the eighth century the western boundary of England was marked by Offa's Dyke, which starts in Gloucestershire: now it is the river Wye, in its spectacular gorges and beautiful wooded valley.

Lucky are those born twixt Severn and Wye,
Too poor to live and too healthy to die.

Few other areas retain the character of the mysterious primeval forest which once covered the country better than the Royal Forest of Dean, situated on high land between the two rivers, fifty square miles (129 sq km) of broadleaved and coniferous woodlands and open country. Alternately nurtured since AD 1016, when Canute declared it a royal hunting forest, and plundered for its natural resources — iron, stone, coal and timber — its industrial heritage is part of this magic and mystery.

These curiosities have been chosen as examples of what can be found. They are listed in an order permitting ease of travel; so you won't get lost, grid references have been quoted using the Ordnance Survey 1:50,000 sheets (Landranger Series).

So come with us on a trip through the valleys where mists lie low and forests dark and mysterious, where surprises are just round the corner.

ACKNOWLEDGEMENTS

We owe our gratitude to the myriad of seldom-named authors of church and district guides who have provided such a wealth of material of interest, and to the untold custodians whose dedicated enthusiasm and affection has ensured the curiosities are maintained, and to those we can name for their personal and generous assistance: Arthur Price of Frocester Court and farm; Noel Hemming, churchwarden of Southam Church of the Ascension; David Storey of Alkerton Grange, Eastington; Mrs H Clifford of Frampton Court, Frampton-on-Severn; Viscount Bledisloe and staff of Lydney Park; the Curator and staff of Gloucester Folk Museum; Leslie Gardiner of Bonusprint who processed every photograph in this book.

Beatrix Potter display, Eastgate Market, Gloucester.

WORMINGTON

DEATH AND RESURRECTION

Location: East of B4078, six miles north-east of Tewkesbury. Sheet 150 03903649

Although for our own interest we may seek out funerary art in all its manifold forms, nowhere are we so conscious of the pathos of death as when it involves an infant in arms. Tudor and Jacobean symbolism enables us to be somewhat objective, but there are some monuments which show mother and child together and which bring lumps to our throats as we reflect on the great sadnesses which were caused so many centuries ago.

Anne Savage died in childbirth in 1605, and a brass in the church, which has the unusual double dedication to both The Holy Trinity and to St. Katherine (who is shown on her wheel in medieval glass within), depicts her with her baby, lying in an Elizabethan fourposter bed complete with curtains and valences:

> *Anne eldest daughter of Richard Daston and wife of John Savage of Nobury, Worcs. 1605 in childbed with infant.*

There is another very interesting and probably unique item in this little church. Hanging over a side altar is a small slab of stone sculpted in bold relief which was excavated from the grounds of Wormington Grange. It is said to have hung originally in Winchcombe Abbey until this was destroyed in 1539, and shows the crucified Lord with the Holy Spirit, in the symbolised form of an outstretched hand above. The sculpture is well over 1,000 years old: the detail and treatment of the tunic, arms and feet indicate a Saxon origin, dated as ninth century work.

Child mortality in this district was much greater than nowadays. Treated in a more flamboyant manner than Anne Savage, at nearby Twyning St. Mary Magdelene's, Sybil Clare had died in 1575 and lies recumbent with her infant, this time carved lifesize in alabaster.

BECKFORD

A WALKER EXTRA-ORDINAIRE

Location: North of the A435, four miles north of Tewkesbury. Sheet 150 97603578

Just to the right of the porch in the churchyard of St. John the Baptist is a headstone in memory of Sarah Dyer, who died in 1838. The inscription reads:

She was daily letter carrier from Beckford to Tewkesbury for 19 years and having walked about 16 miles a day during that period is supposed to have walked about 90,000 miles.

This is interesting enough, but the carvings both inside and outside the church are curious in the extreme. The south doorway is a fine example of mid-twelfth-century mason's skill.

Not for this church the Crucifixion, nor the Agnus Dei, nor even St. Michael slaying the dragon: this tympanum has on either side, animals with five ears and horns, the most odd-looking donkeys with punk hair-styles, an eye, and the Cross with a plump bird standing on its right arm. One interpretation is that it depicts the animal creation adoring the Holy Trinity, the Eye representing the Father, the Cross the Son, and the Dove the Holy Ghost; they may have been carved crudely purposefully to avoid identification with any particular species of animal — in which case the interpretation is correct! More recently an alternative has been put forward based on Celtic art. According to this, the animals are sacred beasts of the Celts and the bird standing on the Cross is a goose, then a sacred bird. These are all paying homage to the new religion represented by the Cross.

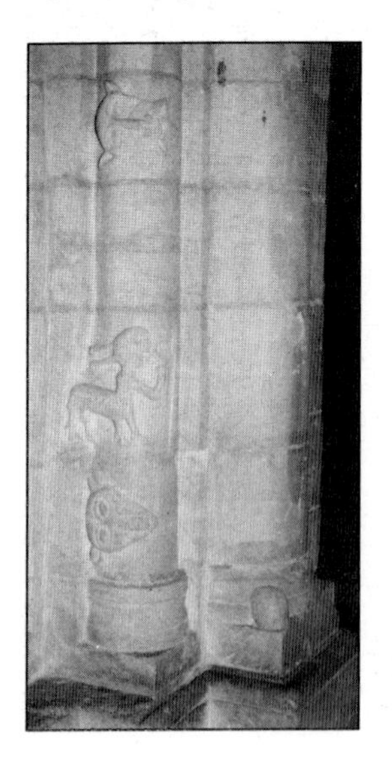

Strange carvings are inside, too. On the nave tower arch, in itself another fine example of twelfth-century Norman work, are carved two demonish heads and a Centaur. This latter is sometimes thought to be part of the badge of King Stephen. But why are they here and what purpose did they serve when they were created with such determination and skill?

OXENTON

WHEELS OF LIFE

Location: Off the A435, three miles east of Tewkesbury. Sheet 150 95853147

Once a possession of the Abbey of Tewkesbury, St. John the Baptist is an almost unspoiled medieval church, though the font and the oak benches are fourteenth century.

The interior seems to have been entirely covered with paintings. The south wall has the remains of three superimposed layers of various periods, the latest being a rare example of the Ten Commandments written in an hinged book.

Wheels of Life were favourite seventeenth and eighteenth century illustrations of Time and Death. There are two wheels painted here. The one under the tower may be a Catherine Wheel, recalling the saint's martyrdom. The other is different and seems to be witness to an ancient superstitious custom once practiced in Oxenton when a cartwheel was wrapped round with straw and dipped in oil or tar and set on fire, and then allowed to roll down the hill behind the church. If it ran true, good fortune would follow for twelve months; if it failed to reach the bottom of the hill, the reverse was expected.

On the north wall of the north aisle, a tablet to the Earl of Ellenborough, who died in 1871, states among other things that his

almost unrivalled powers of oratory were the admiration of the British Senate.

Immediately behind the wall is his mausoleum, which has neither window nor door. Here he is buried with his illegitimate son, Captain Richmond.

TEDDINGTON

AN OLD SIGNPOST AND AN EVEN OLDER MARKER

Location: At the junction of the A438 and the A435. Sheet 150 96403380

Signposts from earlier days often had hands or fingers pointing to significant towns, and sometimes indicating distances in miles. This particular post marked the spot where five roads met and was very important to travellers; it had to be moved a few yards to make way for road improvements, though it retains its original form.

The multi-fingered stone guide-post with pyramidal top and ball-finial was erected by Edmund Attwood in 1676. A small metal plaque bears the inscription:

Edmund Attwood of the Vine Tree
At the first time erected me
And freely he did this bestow
Strange travellers the way to show
Since generations past and gone
Repaired by Charles Attwood of Teddington.

On the opposite side of the busy A435 road and almost in a garage forecourt is another stone, this time even older, a standing monolith with several holes running through it. This is the Tibblestone which derives its name from *Theobald's Stone*, commemorating an early local landowner whose name is preserved also in *Teddington.* The stone marked the meeting-place of the Tibblestone Hundred and is in the classic location: at a crossroads, on an elevated site, and on a parish boundary. Such meeting-places were probably very ancient and could be pre-Saxon, even pre-Roman.

The nearby church of St. Nicholas has a pulpit, sounding board and reading desk of 1655, a most unusual date for church furniture. Incised in the back of the pulpit for all to see are the names of the Commonwealth churchwardens, Michael Tyller and William Attwood (a relative of Edmund, who raised the finger-post), and the desk has carved on it various texts:

Pray continually. Pray without ceasing.
Quench not ye spirit.
Despise not prophecying.

ALSTONE

WALLS DO HAVE EARS!

Location: South of the B4077, three miles east of Tewkesbury. Sheet 150 98373250

Dating from the twelfth century, St. Margaret's church has twice been subject to extensive repairs, but fortunately the 'restorers' did not eliminate its most curious feature.

Centuries ago, sermons lasted for hours and churches had on display, near the pulpit, a timer so that both the preacher and the congregation could estimate the passage of time by the amount of sand left to fall. Did the listeners here use a more subtle method? Behind the pulpit, above the preacher's left shoulder, an ear is sculpted in bold relief on the wall. Why is this here? Was this stone originally being carved to be the head of some saint or king, and the long-departed craftsman, not satisfied with this beginning, threw it away? Or was it perhaps a test piece created by an apprentice? Or a product of whim of the mason, in the tradition of the 'mason's licence' of the times? Nobody knows, only that the stone found itself used, and here it is behind the preacher's head — perhaps a perpetual reminder that his words are not falling on deaf ears, perhaps a warning to him to be brief for almost directly above his head in the little central timber-framed turret hangs the church clock, and its bell. They made their point more clearly in those days!

Placed on the north wall in 1671, is a plain memorial. The verses are of a high quality for so remote a village, though the author is not known:

Here are the attoms of as faire a face
As nature ere fram'd, made fairer yet by grace,
This temple late like Solomon's richly drest
With beauty in itself . . .; more from its queste,
Whose ruins rest in hope here; to Returne
Like Thee more faire and glorious from its Urne,
Thus Shee shall change not dye; ye good n'ere dyes
But like the day star only sets to rise.
Let them with feigned virtues fortify
Their tombes, whose sickly virtues seem to dye.
But spare her tombe, as needless and unsafe
Her virtues shall outlive her Epitaph.

Temporis Ergo posuit T.D. Coniunx Amantissimus.

STANLEY PONTLARGE

FEELING COMFORTABLE?

Location: South of B4077, six miles south-east of Tewkesbury. Sheet 150 99923028

Just as it was believed that medicine had to taste nasty to do some good, so physical pain was considered necessary to enable the spirit to be uplifted. Surely, though, it is advisable to stand through a service in this church, undedicated though worshipped in for over 800 years, than sit in the discomfort offered on these pews? Here, they are slippery with age, their rough-hewn seats only eight inches deep, their backs just high enough to affect adversely the more sensitive of one's lumbar vertebrae, the sloping, sagging kneeling rail almost impossible to balance on, especially as one is likely to slide towards the centre unless one holds tightly to the back of the seat in front.

Now these six pews are relegated to either side of the Norman font which was later cut into octagonal shape, symbolizing re-creation, but earlier worshippers from the village named after the Norman lord Robert Pont de l'Arche (itself a substantial small town on the Seine in Normandy) must have wondered why the craftsmen made them so very unappealing as they squirmed through the long sermons. Perhaps after all that was the intent of the woodworker? Was it a sedentary equivalent of sack-cloth and ashes?

In many Norman churches the chancel arch sags towards one side. An explanation sometimes given is that the arch was constructed that way deliberately to represent the drooping head of Our Lord as He suffered on the cross. Here the chancel arch has to be seen to be believed, for its chevroned curve is flattened by the huge weight of masonry above it, and one side leans out at such an angle that anyone who has not a clear conscience might hesitate to pass underneath.

Please note that the photographer was standing upright!

TODDINGTON

THE MANOR

Location: Off the B4077, eight miles east of Tewkesbury. Sheet 150 03703342

The Tracy family have lived in this area for centuries. It was Sir William Tracy of Toddington who died in 1530 and made such an outrageous Protestant will that when its contents became known the Archbishop of Canterbury ordered that his body be exhumed and burnt at the stake as a heretic. This had the reverse effect to the one required. It was said that Sir William had done

> *. . . more harm to the Christian religion by his death than by his pestiferous contentions before.*

The present Toddington Manor was built between 1820 and 1835 by Sir Charles Hanbury-Tracy on the strength of wealth derived from the Hanbury family's ironworks at Pontypool, of his marriage into the Tracy family in 1798 via Henrietta, daughter and heiress of the 8th Viscount Tracy of Rathcoole, adoption of his bride's surname and acquisition of the manor of Toddington, and of his appointment as chairman of the commission that decided on the plan for the building of the Houses of Parliament in 1835. While at Oxford he had developed an interest in architecture and the Manor was carried out to his own designs at a cost of more than £150,000.

The buildings reflect his fondness for the Gothic style, and incorporate features adopted from Oxford colleges. The exterior presents an array of pointed windows, a battlemented parapet and a wealth of pinnacles and turrets making it easy to accept that Hanbury-Tracy had some influence over the design for the rebuilding of the Houses of Parliament. Aspects of the interior are also Gothic, the library especially resembling that of Horace Walpole at Strawberry Hill; yet in spite of so much stony excellence, the house was warm and comfortable. No trouble or expense was spared to achieve the right effects — fireplaces made of marble with mirrored overmantels, gold leaf used to highlight carved decorations in ceilings and corniches, and medieval glass imported from Europe for the windows.

The Revd. Francis E Witts (1783-1854), rector of Upper Slaughter, whose memories of life in the county, *The Diary of a Cotswold Parson*, throw many delightful insights on those times, recorded:

October 11th, 1823. After calling at Stanway House, where I remained till after luncheon . . . passed near Toddington where the magnificent Gothic mansion of Mr Hanbury Tracy, the exterior of which is now completed, presents a very handsome object from the road. Mr Tracy has combined in this structure, with much judgment and taste, and at very great expense, some of the most interesting morceaux of ancient gothic architecture from Oxford and other places. A tower rises in the centre copied from that of Magdalen College, and the cloister and grand entrance of Christchurch are imitated in the principal part of the mansion; the west window of Tintern Abbey appears in miniature in what is called a chapel return; but in fact is not a chapel, the interior being laid out in domestic apartments.

Ten years later, Witts recorded another visit, and work on the Manor was still continuing.

Hanbury-Tracy paid the same attention to detail in the gardens as to the building itself, and this, combined with his imaginative designs and skill in motivating the local craftsmen, which Witts attributed to

. . . the personal superintendence of Mr Tracy

inspired Verey's claim that

. . . in the history of British domestic architecture, the house stands alone.

In conception, the Manor was a dream being realised, an undertaking only to be entertained by a man of considerable wealth and with the dual aim of inspiring contemporaries and of affording accommodation and facilities not inferior to those found in royal residences. The dream did not last, and for more than four decades the Manor has stood empty and unused.

TREDINGTON

DRAGONS ABOUNDING

Location: East of the A38, two miles south of Tewkesbury. Sheet 150 90502957

Though the main body of the church of St. John the Baptist under the timber-framed tower and spire is Norman in origin, the south porch carries a date-stone of 1624. Here there are two dragons to greet the visitor. Most people concentrate on the Norman doorway arch with its dragon-head stop — one wicked looking beast indeed. But the curious should look downwards, watching where they tread. The muddy seas which created the Lower Lias clay lasted for about ten million years. In them, 180 million years ago, lived many kinds of reptile, including the Ichthyosaurus, which grew up to thirty feet long and was unusual in that it gave birth to live young, not laying eggs. In the paving stones beneath your feet is a fossil of a marine reptile, about nine feet long and believed to be that of just such an Ichthyosaurus dating from those Jurassic times.

Having recovered from the shock, take a rest on the stone seat on the north side of the chancel. This was put there before pews or benches were introduced into churches, and was for the use of the infirm and elderly; hence the expression, often incorrectly applied, that *the weak go to the wall.*

But beware! Outside is a fourteenth-century churchyard cross, tall and slender, and an illustrated Norman tympanum over the blocked north door. Then yet another dragon awaits the unwary. The hinge furniture of the gate takes the shape of a dragon's head, with long snout and vicious teeth, meticulously crafted in iron.

If one dragon doesn't get you, the other will!

STOKE ORCHARD

UNIQUE WALL PAINTINGS

Location: East of the M5, three miles south of Tewkesbury. Sheet 150 91752829

All four walls of the nave of the church of St. James the Great are covered with unique paintings, some dating back to the twelfth century. The earliest are the most important and comprise a cycle that represents the only complete life of St. James still remaining in England. Rather like a strip-cartoon, they tell in lively fashion the adventures of the Apostle, in which he defeats and converts an evil magician, and a scribe called Jeslas. The last of the twenty-eight scenes shows the souls of James and Jeslas being carried to heaven in a napkin.

Most probably this series was painted because Stoke Orchard was on the main pilgrimage route to the shrine of St. James of Compostela in Spain, via the port of Bristol. Though the paintings are often fragmentary and of poor artistic quality, the decorative borders are most striking and in their motifs of Scandinavian origin provide a link with the curious school of sculpture in the Hereford region of Kilpeck, as do some of the animal heads carved around the north door of c.1170. The church also has several scratch-dials for telling the time of Mass before the invention of clocks. Votive crosses have been incised by pilgrims around the south door, possibly before setting off to the shrine of St. James in Spain.

Nearby, Mill Farmhouse has a brick dovecote dated 1741, with a gabled roof and lantern.

ASHCHURCH

HOME TO ROOST

Location: East of M5, two miles south-east of Tewkesbury. Sheet 150 92303080

Fiddington, part of Ashchurch, the *church near the ash tree*, though less than half-a-mile from the M5, is a peaceful hamlet with a fine sixteenth-century timber-framed manor house, once the home of William Ferrars.

Dovecotes were once the living larders of our ancestors and were so important as to be planned as part of the overall design of the estate and built in the same style as the main house. Some still stand, like quaint watchtowers snuggled up beside farm buildings, others set apart like intriguing follies on a hill or in a garden.

In the seventeenth century England boasted over 26,000 dovecotes, leading one visitor to exclaim:

No kingdom in the world has so many dovehouses.

Within a hundred years no farmhouse or country estate was complete without its dovecote: the pigeons within them provided food, fertiliser, medicine, and sporting entertainment, not to mention feathers for stuffing pillows and beds which, according to superstition, would guarantee the sleeper a long life!

Dovecotes — also known as pigeon houses, columbaria and culver houses (*culver* was the Anglo-Saxon word for pigeon) — may have been introduced to Britain by the Romans who were great pigeon breeders, but the earliest known architectural remains date back to Norman times.

In the grounds of Fiddington Manor stands a huge, stone, very fine dove cote with an inscription bearing the date 1637. It has four gables and a cupola and the copings and kneelers carry splendid carved finials.

The pigeons may have had a short life, but they certainly lived here in some style.

TEWKESBURY

ABBEY AND TOWN

Location: At the junction of the A38 and A438. Sheet 150 89103250

The Warwickshire Avon falls into the Severn here, and on the sides of both, for many miles back, there are the finest meadows that were ever seen. In looking over them and beholding the endless flocks and herds, one wonders what can become of all that meat!

So wrote Cobbett in 1820 in praise of the fertility of Tewkesbury soil. The town is in the Vale, but so dependent were the early fortunes of many Cotswold manors on the monastic masters of Tewkesbury that they can scarcely be separated.

Tewkesbury Abbey was a powerful landowner: its manor spread over the Cotswold hills as far as Fairford. The enormous tithe barn at Stanway gives some idea of the volume of tithes stowed there for the abbot; the fact that rustlers stole 1,000 head of the Abbey flock from Stanway in 1340 illustrates the scale on which the Abbey farmed its sheep. So fertile was the soil surrounding the Abbey that the monks grew grapes on what are still known as the Vineyards, and owned two mills; one still exists on the Mill Avon, cut by the monks in the twelfth century to power their mill.

The town was already a royal borough by Domesday, and although it participated in the wool industry it did not rise or fall on these fortunes as did smaller hill-towns. Situated on the navigable confluence of the Severn and Avon, Tewkesbury had the advantage of water transport years before roads were improved. This was the way the stone came for its mighty Benedictine Abbey, brought from Caen in Normandy by sea and river.

The Abbey Church of St. Mary is built on cathedral proportions, with the largest surviving Norman central tower in the world dominating the town's roofscape. It can be admired not just because it is fine-looking but because of the devotion of past parishioners in keeping it that way. Every parish struggles to preserve the fabric of its church, but in Tewkesbury's case the townspeople were determined to save the Abbey from desecration and destruction after the suppression of the monastery. Having been accustomed to using the western part of the nave for worship, they approached Henry VIII through his commissioners and petitioned him for permission to purchase the whole building for use as a parish church. The King charged them the value of the metal in the bells and the lead on the roof, the very considerable sum of £453 — but at least they could have the church lock, stock and pulpit. To their credit, the townsfolk raised this sum in two years, and thus they were able to preserve the splendid, sturdy Norman tower, the nave, and the six-fold arch in the west front, the largest of its kind in Britain.

The curiosity-seeker will be kept busy inside. This must be one of the few churches in the country with reason to thank Oliver Cromwell, since it was he who first got the so-called Milton organ, one of the three here, on the move. During the Commonwealth he had it taken from Magdalen College, Oxford, for which it was made, and installed in the chapel of his Hampton Court quarters. There his Latin Secretary, the aspiring poet John Milton, strummed the odd toccata on it for his master's delectation, as before his blindness he was a keen musician and able organist. The name has stuck ever since. The organ later went back to Magdalen College, to be brought to Tewkesbury in 1737.

The word 'curious' applies also to some of the monuments in this church. The Wakeman Cenotaph is a wonderful representation of the medieval preoccupation with death. But how did this monument get its name? Every thing about it is wrong. The tomb is a grisly memento mori depicting a decaying cadaver of a monk in an open shroud as it might appear a little time after death, crawled over by five vermin, a worm, snake, frog, rat and snail or spider, all feasting on the corpse. According to the convention of the time, this effigy should be at ground level, with another in full ecclesiastical vestments occupying the upper level — the form of medieval ecclesiastical monument to illustrate the transitoriness of earthly things: *Sic transit gloria Mundi*

The origin of the tradition which gives this tomb its name is not known but it seems unlikely that there is any genuine connection with John Wakeman, the last abbot. There is no inscription or epitaph as such to help us. There are no clues either in its design or sculpting. Indeed, it is of architectural style of the mid-fifteenth century, a hundred years earlier than the death of Wakeman. We know that after the dissolution of the monastery in 1539, Wakeman was granted a pension and acquired the nearby manor of Forthampton, with its fine Tudor house, where he was buried in 1549, though after having been created the first bishop of the new diocese of Gloucester in 1541. So just whose tomb is it?

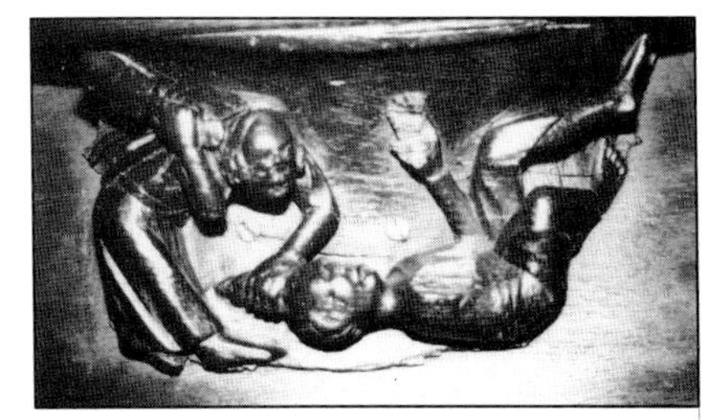

Though the stellar vaulting of the chancel roof is quite breath-taking, with its circles of gilded suns, the emblems of the House of York, put there to commemorate their victory over the Lancastrians here in 1471, do not neglect to look downwards, and especially at the carved misericords. Regrettably most have been mutilated but those to the north depict domestic, farmyard and bucolic scenes, and mythical creatures from the medieval Bestiaries; the only one remaining on the south shows a religious scene.

Now explore beyond the Abbey church. Tewkesbury is one of the finest half-timbered towns in England, with spectacular overhanging eaves, a labyrinth of medieval alleys, fascinating old inns and an ancient mill. The wide river and low-lying flood meadows restricted a sprawling growth and resulted in backfilling behind older buildings. The resultant narrow entrances have made Tewkesbury a place of secret alleyways: an early Baptist chapel of 1623 is tucked away in one, beyond the shadow of the great Abbey. One of the oldest Non-conformist chapels in the country, it retains some old features, late seventeenth-century furnishings, panelled pulpit and gallery.

Mill Street leads down to the Mill Avon water-front and the site of the Abbey Mills. Now an early nineteenth-century building, it was renamed Abel Fletcher's Mill after the Quaker tanner in *John Halifax, Gentleman* for which it was the original; Tewkesbury is the *Nortonbury* of Mrs Craik's famous Victorian novel. Under her maiden name, Miss Mulcock, she had visited the town in 1825 and taken lunch at The Bell, a twelfth-century former hostelry originally within the Abbey's grounds for visiting monks and pilgrims, and decided to make the inn feature in her novel: *John Halifax*, too, lunched here. Another famous literary figure stayed just a few yards along the street: Dicken's *Mr Pickwick* rested at the Hop Pole Hotel and warmed himself by the fire; a plaque outside celebrates the occasion.

One wonders what the House of Nodding Gables in the High Street was called before a supporting timber gave way and caused one of the two gables to lean over sideways? Its fine old frontage of four overhanging storeys on carved brackets, leaded casements and oriel windows, now sports a modern appendage: a large golden key indicates that a Building Society occupies the ground floor.

This is not the only item of street furniture in the commercial area of the town. On the corner of St. Mary's Lane, no. 100 Church Street has an early nineteenth-century sign of a huge beadle's hat, suspended from the first floor.

The Mythe (Old English for river confluence) was not mentioned in the Domesday Book, but by 1327 was recorded as having ten taxable inhabitants. King John's Castle is a more recent name for Mythe Manor House which is more likely to have been associated with the Abbey than with a residence for King John, who when he visited would have occupied the now vanished Holme Castle. Certainly it belonged to Gilbert de Clare, 6th Earl of Gloucester: when he died he left the manor to the Abbey, and it was used as a rest house for the monks of Tewkesbury, Fairford and Thornbury until 1539. Then John Wakeman, the wily abbot, succeeded in establishing his brother Richard there just prior to the dissolution, and it remained in Wakeman hands for the next 300 years. All the original buildings of the manor house were pulled down, except for the large square rubble staircase tower whose massive walls rise to three storeys. Against the west face a gabled wing with mullioned and transomed windows was added in the seventeenth century and make it one of the most interesting and delightful of the town's residences.

Mythe Bridge is a splendid example of the design and work of Thomas Telford, built between 1823 and 1826 of cast iron with a single span of 170 feet. Either side of the road is a toll house. One is a small hexagon collecting house, while opposite is a charming building with a single storey collecting house facing the road but other storeys below road level at the back.

FORTHAMPTON

HARSH PUNISHMENTS

Location: South of the A438, two miles west of Tewkesbury. Sheet 150 85873250

The village is dominated by its manor house and church. Forthampton Court was the residence of the abbots of Tewkesbury, and though alterations have been carried out through the centuries,, it still retains the magnificent Banqueting Hall of 1380, the Abbot's Chapel and a thirteenth-century picture on wood of Edward the Confessor and the Pilgrim. In 1539 at the dissolution of the monastery, Henry VIII took possession and gave John Wakeman, the last abbot, the Court as his residence, first having appointed him the new Bishop of Gloucester. Since Wakeman's death in 1549, and his burial at the altar of St. Mary's nearby, many illustrious families have been in occupation.

The church is an ancient building which retains its original stone altar or mensa, one of only three which survived *in situ* at the time of the Reformation of 1538.

But life for the majority of parishioners was hard in this 'Farmstead associated with Forthelm' (a Saxon personal name), and punishments swift and harsh. On a space below the churchyard are preserved the stocks and whipping posts with iron manacles and seating for three — not currently in use! The ancient village pond is nearby but fortunately the ducking stool and posts rotted away years ago.

Other churches in the vicinity have kept interesting curiosities. St. Michael's, Tirley, has a unique clock, made locally from scrap agricultural implements, while at St. John the Baptist, Chaceley, is a large drum thought to be a relic of the church band: here the stocks are kept inside.

Perhaps the villagers of Forthampton have in mind that they will be used again in the near future.

DEERHURST

THE FINEST SAXON BUILDINGS

Location: West of the A38, four miles south of Tewkesbury. Sheet 150 87002991

Here on the banks of the Severn, in a village whose name means *forest of the wild animals*, are two outstanding buildings. A remarkable survival from Saxon days, they provide us with a link to the very origins of our Christian heritage. The village site itself is significant, being on an earlier frontier of Roman Britain, at a point where, traditionally, the river was once fordable.

A monastery was founded at Deerhurst when Aethelric bequeathed lands in 804, and it expanded quickly to become the chief monastery of the ancient Saxon kingdom of Hwicce. Parts of the church of St. Mary, one of the finest Anglo-Saxon churches in Britain, and the only surviving Saxon monastic church, date from that time. Following the Viking invasions the church was restored in the tenth century, and at one time the Benedictine monastery owned 30,000 acres, mainly in Gloucestershire. A measure of Deerhurst's importance in pre-Conquest England was indicated when it gave its name to a treaty and solemn pact of friendship drawn up in 1016 by the English king Edmund Ironside and Cnut the Dane. They divided England between them and fixed the amount to be paid to Cnut's army. Later that year Edmund died and Cnut became King of all England.

The church has many unique features. Dating from the late ninth century is the finest Saxon tub font in existence with its Celtic motifs. Its recent history is one of good fortune. For a lengthy period the bowl was used as a washing tub on a farm until in 1844 Bishop Wilberforce bought it for Longdon church, where it remained for twenty-five years. Then the stem, which bears the same pattern, was found at Apperley Court, and the two were re-united here in Deerhurst.

There are other delights. The eighth-century carved Madonna Panel of the Virgin and Child in the entrance door is startling in its stark simplicity, almost abstract in its modelling. Here the child in the womb is being commemorated rather than a baby in arms — perhaps the finest surviving example of Saxon sculpture.

On the ruined tenth-century apse is the Deerhurst Angel, with its enormous staring eyes, stylised wings and hair suggesting strikingly Celtic influences. Some have even seen analogies with the illumination of the Book of Kells.

The nave capitals of c.1200 are carved to an exceptional standard and contain, interspersed with foliage pattern, human heads, one grinning unselfconsciously, the other two solemn.

On the outside wall is a carving of a dragon's head, said to recall a local legend of a dragon that terrorised the area before being killed by John Smith, a blacksmith, for which he was rewarded with an estate by the king. Other beasts' heads, mysterious, snarling and unique are either side of the middle chancel arch.

This priory church has several fine brasses one of c.1400 depicting St. Anne teaching the Virgin to read but of particular interest is that of Sir John Cassey and his wife. Sir John died in 1400 and was, the inscription says, *Chief Baron of the Exchequer to Our Lord the King*, in this case Richard II. He is dressed in judges' robes and his feet rest on a lion as befits a great officer of state. Dame Alice stands beside him dressed in the high-necked fashion of her day and her feet on a small dog. Below the dog its name *Terri*, or perhaps *Cerri*, is incised: the only example in England of a named pet depicted on a medieval brass.

Deerhurst is unique in having yet another remarkable pre-Conquest building. Odda's Chapel is perhaps the most complete small Anglo-Saxon church now surviving, although its existence so near St. Mary's, only 200 yards down the lane and nearer the river, was unknown until just over 100 years ago. Though dedicated by Ealdred in 1056, it was 'lost' until, during repairs in 1885 to what was regarded as an ordinary half-timbered house, an ancient window was brought to light. A stone window-head was then discovered, inscribed *In honour of the Holy Trinity this Altar has been dedicated.* This provided a link with a large stone found near the building in 1675, after a storm blew down an apple tree and the Odda Stone was discovered entangled in its roots. Translation of its Latin inscription enabled the chapel to be dated precisely — a unique fact for a pre-Conquest building — with a dedication in the Second of the Ides of April in the fourteenth year of the reign of King Edward of the English: on 12 April, 1056.

HASFIELD

THE POWER OF LOVE

Location: East of the A417, six miles west of Tewkesbury. Sheet 162 82622750

Some tombs can be singled out by their contents rather than by their design or construction. Here is one of them.

Situated near the Hasfield Ham, a stretch of green covering a meander of the Severn, Hasfield Court was owned by the Pauncefoote family for almost four centuries from 1200 to 1598, when they were obliged to sell owing to the persecution of recusants — not the mid-Victorian Neo-Renaissance Court there now but a Tudor one on the same site overlooking the river. Dorothy Pauncefoote was born and lived here until she married: nothing remarkable about that as she enjoyed the leisured life of the landed wealthy of the time. She attended the local church, St. Peter's, marvelled at its fifteenth-century carved bench-ends, and her tomb-chest, dated 1568, lies here still, again unremarkable with an inscription around the lid and shields of arms in the panelled sides.

Do not be deceived though by this seeming ordinariness, for a severed hand features in the life of Dorothy Pauncefoote.

Her lover, Julian, was captured by pirates and fell into the clutches of a female Captain Bluebeard who demanded that he marry her. Julian gamely declined, explaining that there was a maid at home who would give her right hand to have him back. He must have wished he hadn't for his captor sneeringly seized upon this cliche: she would only exchange him for Dorothy's hand! Unhesitatingly, Dorothy did what she saw was necessary, and in consequence Julian returned home and married her, no doubt promising volubly to be more judicious in his use of English in the future.

If this story stretches our belief to its limit, then be warned: in the last century Dorothy's tomb was opened and from the remains uncovered it seems it could all be true.

HARTPURY

AN ANCIENT BEE BOLE

Location: On the A417, five miles north-west of Gloucester. Sheet 162 79642530

Before 1851, when hives were first used, colonies of bees were housed in straw skeps. To shelter them from the weather, recesses were built into house walls and outbuildings, known as bee boles.

A rare medieval bee bole stood originally at Nailsworth but was dismantled in the late 1960s and re-erected at Hartpury College. It is now a Grade II listed structure.

Twenty-eight hives were accommodated in it, far more than an ordinary householder would need, and its outstandingly fine crafting in Caen stone and elaborate decoration are clear evidence that it belonged to an owner of wealth and rank. Indeed, at some time in the past it has been reduced in size, and might originally have held as many as thirty-six hives.

So who did it belong to? In the settlements which followed the Conquest in 1066, the two manors of Minchinhampton and Avening became the personal property of William and his Queen, Matilda. In 1087 the Domesday Book recorded tributes of honey, measured in sextaries, as part of these manorial rents. By then, Queen Matilda had founded in Minchinhampton a convent of nuns as a daughter house of the Abbaye aux Dames in Caen. It is likely that the bee bole was constructed by the convent in Minchinhampton in order to produce honey, wax and mead both for its own use and that of the mother house in Caen. Certainly, each autumn the Steward of the convent made the journey to Outrisham, the port for Caen, to take revenues of the two English manors to the mother house.

Though of a later date, there is another interesting piece of our heritage in this village. A short distance from the bridge over the Leadon is Hartpury Mill, its great iron wheel with wooden paddles still in place, its glassy millpond draped in weeping willows.

Within the traditional pattern of manor, church and home farm is a superb fourteenth-century tithe barn, still very much part of a working farm. Its massive roof timbers with braced tiebeams carrying king posts support heraldic finials on the gable-ends, its thick walls buttressed, and enormous doorway just as it was when last used by the abbots of St. Peter's, Gloucester. The abbots maintained accurate records of the enormous number of tithes needed to fill this barn, but other records of village residents are curiously vague. In the church of St. Mary is a plaque to Thomas Biddle Junr.: we are not told when he died but he was interred on 7 Oct, 1728, and that he was *aged 31 years and upwards!* Even so he was sadly missed:

O Cruel Death to take him hence so soon —
To let his Sone goe downe before 'twas noone:
His life was much desir'd with weeping eyes
But oh all is in vaine when God denies.

In the churchyard, the Soper tomb is actually listed Grade II, and displays on the table top a cadaver wrapped in a shroud.

Nearby, a headstone records a most unfortunate occurrence, when John Hale, a blacksmith, was killed in Newent in 1692 whilst engaged in his favourite leisure pursuit:

Loe here's interr'd the Muses Passive Friend
Their Noblest Science — Ringing — was his End
His Actions just. A Martyr of that Skill
Crusht by a Bell 'twas Heavens Sacred Will.
Melodious Bells delighting him on Earth
Exchanged Terrestriall for Celestriall Mirth
This Fatal Stroke in haste did stop his Breath
Lamented was his Unexpected Death.

CORSE AND STAUNTON

GARDEN OF EDEN — LOST AGAIN

Location: On the A417, six miles north-west of Gloucester. Sheet 150 79302950

As one of the several early Victorian experiments in social engineering, this village was chosen for a settlement of workers by Feargus O'Connor, who in 1845 set up the Chartist Co-operative Land Society. O'Connor was a member of the Chartist movement campaigning for electoral reform, but went further than his fellows and planned a utopian world, hopefully ordered, where every family would have its own house and grow its own vegetables. O'Connor's dream was to buy land in rural villages and divide it into equal-sized plots each with a four-roomed bungalow, and then persuade some of the downtrodden industrial workers of those times to be his tenants.

Encouraged by his friend the Vicar, he obtained land at Snig's End for this purpose. Eighty four-roomed brick bungalows, identical in appearance with a low pediment over the central door, were built in groups along the main road. Each had a plot of a few acres and an outbuilding for a pig, and here, O'Connor dreamt, every tenant would rediscover the dignity of living close to the land and earn a living from his own small patch.

One surprise in the centre of this development is to come upon the public house, the Prince of Wales. It looks just like an enlarged version of the Chartist cottages and was built to serve as the school and administrative headquarters of the estate. But it was never used as such and by 1870 had become this public house.

Feargus O'Connor was a man of great energy. At the same time as houses were being built at Snig's End, others were being erected under his Chartist Co-operative scheme at Lowbands, a couple of miles away. Here too a school was built in identical pattern, but this time was taken over by the County Council and used for its original purpose.

One of the original settlers on the Lowbands estate, a Mr How, described the scheme.

In the year 1845 the well-known Chartist agitator Feargus O'Connor and a Manchester solicitor of the name of Roberts were the promoters of the Land Society. The objects were to purchase land in large quantities, to divide each estate into 2, 3 and 4 acre allotments, on which cottages were to be built, the land cultivated for the reception of its members, and from £15 to £30 aid money given to each allottee on location, subject to a perpetual fee farm rent-charge. These promises and objects seemed to people unacquainted with farming so tempting that in the course of a few months 70,000 members had subscribed more than £100,000. Farms were purchased and cottages built in different parts of the country. One of these farms is the Lowbands estate, which consists of about 160 acres, divided into 46 allotments. The members who had subscribed £2.12s.0d, £3.15s.0d, or £5.4s.0d, were entitled to ballot for location in August, 1847. The allottees took possession of their cultivated farms and received the aid-money promised besides a further loan of similar amounts. In September, 1848, one year's rent-charge was due and demand made for it, but the great results promised by farming these small allotments had by this time proved a delusion, and no rent could be paid by any one of the occupants from the produce of the land.

Poor Feargus! His Garden of Eden collapsed, beset with problems but not least the discontent of his latter-day Adams and Eves who could not adapt to a life close to the land. Though the experiment failed, the little houses have survived, now privately owned, some almost unrecognisable with alterations, extensions, pebble-dashing and fancy front doors. Those in The Crescent are listed Grade II and have become part of our national heritage. In Moat Lane, one house bears, on the trefoil over the door, the inscription:

O'Connor Villa. June 12, 1848

This is the month and year of the founder's bankruptcy.

UPLEADON

CURIOSITIES ABOUNDING

Location: East of A4215, ten miles north-west of Gloucester. Sheet 162 76902696

The church of St. Mary the Virgin is probably well over a thousand years old, and stands on a huge mound of clay. The builders may have adapted a man-made raised site of ancient worship; they certainly needed to safeguard the church from flooding of the surrounding marshland along the river Leadon.

Though there are Saxon features it is the Norman and Tudor work for which the church is unique. The twelfth-century north doorway is a fine example of the craftsmanship of that period. The chevron moulded arch encloses a sculpted tympanum depicting the Agnus Dei between two beasts or grotesque creatures: the symbolism is of the triumph of Christ and His Sacrifice amid the evils and dangers of the temporal world. An odd protrusion from one of the arch-mouldings of the doorway appears to be of a human face, no doubt the product of whim of the mason, in the tradition of the 'mason's licence' of the times.

Some time c.1500 the half-timbered tower was added. Whilst there are many timber and half-timbered church towers in Britain, this one, preserving the original main timbers, is half-timbered right from ground-base up throughout its height, and so is unique. The main framing members are of oak, exceptionally long, and painstakingly adzed to an especially smooth finish. The great arching cross-bracing beams, of natural convexity, spring from the main uprights and are pinned in 'wish-bone construction'.

When viewed from outside, the tower is a separate unit of construction. Its vertical lines of long closely-set studding timbers give the appearance of enhanced height, a clever device from the best architectural planners of the period. That no bracing is visible on the exterior enhances still further the appearance of height, a trick often used successfully for this purpose in early Tudor domestic design. When one is inside, the confluence of nave and tower-space equally cleverly produce the impression of the whole being one large nave unit. The tower windows are rare as their traceried mullions are also of wood.

Behind the chancel arch, high on the wall, is a carving of a head of a pig. Why here? There are several possible reasons. It may be an example of contemporary symbolism, for the sow and farrow were used to indicate a selected holy place. It may indicate some link with boar hunting: where the boar roamed man could find food and the place must have the blessing of God's Providence. Certainly the pig was connected in ancient legend with the 'agency of God' for the founding of new sites; it is possible there may have been some link between such beliefs and the origin of the legend concerning the founding of Rome.

The church has a very rare treasure. In 1604, at the Hampton Court Conference, when the opposing views of the clergy of the Established Church and Puritan divines were argued before the King, James I acceded to a request for a new and uniform English translation of the Bible. The completed work was given royal ratification and the 'Authorised Version' was issued in 1611. By Royal Patent of Elizabeth I, only the King's Printer, Robert Barker, could carry out this work. The Bible in this church, known as a *Black Letter Bible* on account of the black typeface employed, is such an edition, prefaced with genealogical and other tables and guide notes, printed by Barker — the New testament in 1611 and the Old Testament in 1613. Barker was unfortunately ruined when the 1631 edition was issued because one of his employees had missed out a vital word: the *Wicked Bible* rendered Exodus 20.14 *Thou shalt commit adultery*. It has been suggested that it was a deliberate attempt to sabotage the Authorised Version, but if so, it failed.

Between two tabletombs to the north-east of the vestry is an interesting epitaph to a local blacksmith, which in accordance with contemporary custom is replete with symbolism relating his occupation to the imagery of death:

In Memory of James Broadtock
Blacksmith, who died Jany. 31st
1768 Aged near 50 years
My sledge and hammer he's reclined
My bellows too has lost its wind
My fire extinct my forge decayed
And in the dust my vice is laid
My coal is burnt my iron's gone
My nails is drove thy work is done

REDMARLEY D'ABITOT

A THEATRICAL ROYAL CONNECTION

Location: On the A417, nine miles north-west of Gloucester. Sheet 150 75243136

Reap wheat, and mow barley,
say the bells of Redmarley.

This village sitting on its hilltop derives its curious name, which in Saxon times was *Reode* [or *Ryde*] *mare leah*, from a number of sources: the thick, sticky, red clay, the red marle, on which it is built; being a border parish at the extreme end of the County and Diocese; and the Norman lords of the manor, the d'Abitot family who came with the Conqueror from near Havre.

Additionally, the village has very unusual names for two of its three streets, which recall its London theatrical connection. Lilly Langtry, the first publicly acknowledged mistress of Albert Edward, Prince of Wales, later King Edward VII, lived here for a short time during her days as actress and royal mistress, at the bottom of the street which became known as Drury Lane. At the top of the hill another street recalls her connection, with the name Hyde Park Corner.

Fascinating as this connection is, do not neglect matters spiritual. An interesting brass behind the organ of the church is inscribed:

All flesh is grasse, wormes meat and clay, and here it hath short time to live, for proofe wheerof both night and day all mortal wights ensamples give beneath this stone fast closde in clay doth sleepe the corpse of George Shipside, wch Christ shall rayse on ye last day and them with Him be glorifide, whose soule now lives assuredly in heaven with Christ our Saviour in perfect peace most joyfully with God's elect for evermore.

Obiit 31 die De bris An. D'ni 1609, Ac.An.AEtatis sue 84. Ecce quid eris.

When translated this becomes: *he died on the 31st day of December in the year of Our Lord 1609, and in the year of his age 84. See what thou wilt be.*

PAUNTLEY

TRACE A LEGEND TO ITS SOURCE

Location: South of the M50, nine miles west of Tewkesbury. Sheet 150 74902890

Turn again Whittington,
Thrice Mayor of London.

The most popular figure of pantomime and fable is the poor orphan country lad who, hearing that the streets of London are paved with gold, bravely makes his way there to seek his fortune. Why it came to be told of Sir Richard Whittington is a mystery, for his was certainly not a rags to riches story. None the less the tale of the medieval 'pest controller' has delighted generation upon generation . . . and starts here.

The Whittingtons came into possession of the manor of Pauntley in 1311 by marriage, and Richard's father, Sir William de Whittington, inherited it in 1332. Little is actually known about Richard's early life. Certainly he was born here, but the date is not known precisely, so we can only say 'about 1358'. Sir William and Dame Joan had three sons, the youngest of whom became a mercer in London, later a merchant-financier — amongst his frequent loans to the Crown was one for the enormous sum of £6,400 to Henry VI — three times Mayor (there was no such post of Lord Mayor, then) of London, in 1397, 1406, and 1419 — and Dick of pantomime fame. His elderly father died while Richard was young, so that part of the story that Dick was brought up by his widowed mother is true, though in reality they lived in considerable comfort. He married Alice Fitzwarren, daughter of Sir Ivor, not a London merchant as in the tale but a country gentleman of considerable estate in the south-west of England.

When in 1862 the carved figure of a boy holding some sort of animal was found in the foundations of a house in Westgate Street, Gloucester, it was hailed as 'Dick and his cat', and the idea got about that it had given rise to the story. This though is doubtful.

Pauntley Court continued in Whittington ownership until 1545, and part of the present house dates from the sixteenth century. There is a very interesting fifteenth-century dovecote, four-square with gables, which gives some idea of the scale of the Tudor manor.

DYMOCK

TWO AUTHORS — A CURSE AND A POEM

Location: On the B4216, twelve miles north-west of Gloucester. Sheet 149 32147188

In 1892 a lead tablet was found in a small cupboard in Wilton Place, providing clear evidence that witchcraft was practiced in the area. The inscription on the tablet lays a curse on Sarah Ellis, whose name is written, significantly, backwards at the top. Symbols representing the good and evil spirits of the moon are followed by the figures 3 6 9 — the mystical number of the moon, and whose inclusion added to the strength of the charm's influence. Then the demons Hasmodat, Acteus, Magalesius, Ormenus, Lieus, Nicon, Mimon, and Zeper are called upon to

> *. . . make this person to Banish away from this place and countery Amen to my desier Amen.*

Neither Sarah Ellis nor the commissioner of the curse have ever been identified, but local legend says that Sarah was affected so adversely that she committed suicide and was buried at a crossroads with a stake in her heart. Certainly there is an Ellis' Cross on the boundary of the parishes of Dymock and Oxenhall, about two-and-a-half miles from Wilton Place. The curse belongs to the second half of the seventeenth century and was probably based on Henry Cornelius Agrippa's *Three Books of Occult Philosophy*, published first in 1532 and translated into English in 1651. The demons come straight from Anglo-Saxon folklore and the epic poem *Beowulf.* Generations of country-folk familiar with the Bible would have no difficulty identifying such a dragon in the Book of Revelations.

Just before the First World war, from 1911, Dymock was home to many of the eminent poets of the day. Lascelles Abercrombie, Wilfred Gibson, Edward Thomas, John Drinkwater and Rupert Brooke lived in the area, and were joined by Robert Frost. The famous *War Sonnets* were published from this village, and included Brooke's *The Soldier.*

> *If I should die, think only this of me . . .*

The war, in which Brooke and Thomas died, caused the break-up of the Dymock Poets.

An indisputably unique epitaph can be found in St. Mary the Virgin's churchyard:

> *Too sweeter babes yeun nare did see*
> *Than God amitly give to Wee*
> *But they were ortaken wee aguefits*
> *And here they lives as dead as Wits.*

SOUTHAM

FOR A WIFE, FRIENDS AND COLLEAGUES

Location: Three miles north-east of Cheltenham, on the B4632. Sheet 163 96982568

The Southam estate was bought in 1833 by Edward Law, the first and last Earl of Ellenborough, Governor General of India from 1841 to 1844, and renamed Southam de la Bere as he claimed descent from a previous owner of 1607, Richard de la Bere, whose own ancestor had fought with the Black Prince and was given the right to include the Prince of Wales' feathers in his coat of arms. Ellenborough found the church as a derelict ruin, and drastically 'restored' it in neo-Norman style as a private chapel in memory of his first wife, Octavia, dedicating it The Church of The Ascension.

His influence is everywhere. In neo-Norman niches are his own bust (he died in 1871) and that of Octavia, who had died fifty-two years earlier. Neither are buried here: he, along with his illegitimate son, is in a door-less, window-less mausoleum at Oxenton, four miles away; she lies at North Cray, Kent.

Brightly coloured heraldic and decorative stained glass is mostly in memoriam to Ellenborough's military friends and his relations, especially his three brothers who were all bishops. In the nave is a bronze equestrian memorial to the Duke of Wellington, another friend, who took the waters at Cheltenham.

Many of the furnishings came from abroad, reflecting the Earl's eclectic taste, though some of the items sit oddly in the Norman surroundings: for example the font is a bird-bath from India. A major curiosity are the three foreign fourteenth-century Renaissance-design choir stalls with carved misericords depicting mermaids, lions, Neptune, Satan, and winged animals' heads.

Much remains of the original early sixteenth-century manor house, though a good deal of remodelling has taken place to fit its present use as a hotel. Amongst other structures, Ellenborough built the Summer House to commemorate the staff who served him in India during his time as Governor General. It is a curious square stone building with pendant Gothic cusping under a hipped roof.

PRESTBURY

THE PHENOMENAL FRED ARCHER

Location: On the A46, one mile north of Cheltenham. Sheet 163 97002390

Prestbury lies under the great shelf of Cleeve Hill. Its roots go back beyond Domesday, and its name means *the priest's fortified place.* As early as 1249 Prestbury was granted a borough charter, but it never expanded into a prosperous market town because of its proximity to Cheltenham.

Now the home of the National Hunt festival, racing history began last century, first on Cleeve Hill but transferred to 'Cheltenham' as a three-day event in 1819, on land belonging to Prestbury Park, and only six years later was attracting as many as 40,000 people.

Prestbury's own phenomenal son of the turf,

> *the greatest wonder that ever crossed a horse,*

was born in 1857, either above a stable backing onto the derelict chapel graveyard or, according to a plaque, in St. George's Place. There is no such dispute about where the legendary Fred Archer received his early riding lessons. The King's Arms at Prestbury retains in the bar a shoe from his first mount, and a plaque stating unequivocally:

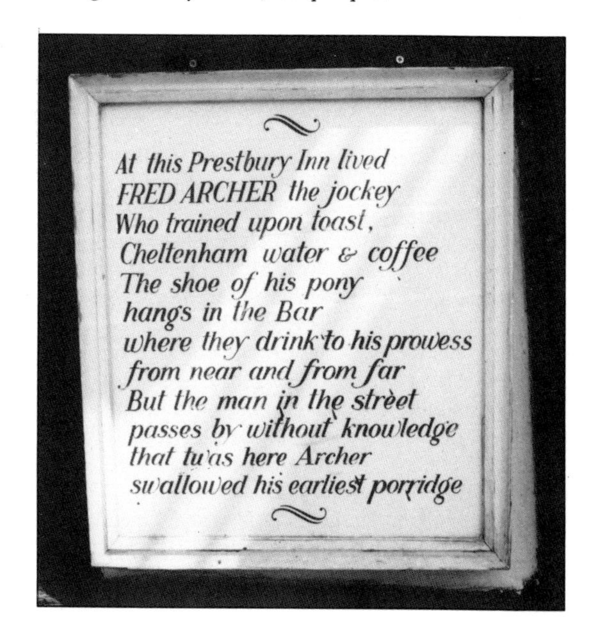

CHELTENHAM

THE MERRIEST SICK RESORT ON EARTH

Location: At the junction of the A40, A46 and A435. Sheet 163 95272267

Cheltenham spreads along a terrace under the great bluff of Cleeve Hill and above the flat vale watered by the Severn. *Pretty, poor and proud* is a local maxim to describe this town.

It is pretty. The Promenade has been described as the most beautiful boulevard in Britain. Inspired by the Trevi Fountains in Rome, Neptune's Fountain of 1893 draws water from the river Chelt below the 'Prom'. It is not poor: rather it is smart, fashionable and, on the surface, prosperous. Proud it certainly is: Cheltenham succeeded where others in the area failed. To the three Ps should be added a fourth — for the success story of Cheltenham began with pigeons. In what was in 1716 a meadow outside the little town (and is now the Ladies College) a number of pigeons were seen pecking at salt crystals at a spring. Realising the potential, the owner, William Mason, a local hosier, railed in the spot, raised a thatched shed over it and gave Cheltenham its first pump room. His astute son-in-law, Henry Skillicorne, built a more permanent and presentable edifice in 1748 to house the spring, improved the approach to it and called it a Spa.

Physicians wrote long treatises on the medicinal virtues of the waters, prescribing them to their wealthy clients for a variety of disorders from constipation, rheumatism and gout to '*scrofulous afflictions, exudation and worms*'. George III stamped them with the royal seal of approval by 'taking' them in a five-week holiday here in 1788. On the other hand, William Cobbett saw the town as a sink for plunderers and drunkards and debauchees of all descriptions, but what he called *the merriest sick resort on earth* prospered. New wells were sunk, the Spa waters flowed, visitors arrived by the coach- and train-load, and the town put the pigeons in its coat-of-arms: they appear also on the new finger-posts giving directions to modern visitors.

Anyone who wishes to know more about Cheltenham could do no better than read Henry Skillicorne's epitaph in the twelfth-century parish church of St. Mary, one of the longest in any English church, a potted biography as well as a eulogy, and a virtual history of the town.

Even in an age of long-winded, pompous memorials it seems excessive, but ends simply:

He lived and dyed an honest man.

No man could ask for more, but whether taking the waters for medicinal or for social purposes, caring for one's health here could be a dangerous business. A whole family died, so they claim in the same church, from unnatural means:

Here I lie with my two daughters,
Who died through drinking Cheltenham waters,
If only we had stuck to Epsom salts
We should not be lying in these here vaults.

A wall plaque records another unnatural death, that of Mrs Katherine A'Court, who was poisoned by her footman, Joseph Armstrong, in 1776. Her monument tells the whole story in fourteen lines, the last five of which read:

Beloved from infancy by a tender husband
In whose arms she died an unnatural death effected by poison
Administered by the hands of a cruelly wicked Livery Servant
Whose resentment at being detected in theft
Prompted him to perpetuate this horrid and execrable crime.

The man was tried, found guilty and hanged at Gloucester.

A quaint inscription on a tombstone outside reads:

To the memory of John Higgs, died 1825
Here lies John Higgs,
A famous man for killing pigs,
For killing pigs was his delight
Both morning, afternoon and night
Both heats and cold he did endure,
Which no physician could e'er cure;
His knife is laid, his work is done,
I hope to heaven his soul has gone.

A further enigmatic epitaph reads:

To the memory of Isaac Ballinger, died 1721.
Reader! pray covet not this world,
Out of it you may soon be hurled,
For as a wheel it turns about,
And it was a wheel that turned me out.

While you are seeking out these tombstones, let your eyes wander upwards from time to time, and you will see the most elaborate and beautiful iron lamp standards.

Amidst the High Street hub-hub are two pieces of public art — the Wishing Fish Clock and the Stampeding Elephants mural. When the Regent Arcade opened, the renowned artist and craftsman Kit Williams, who lives in the Cotswolds, agreed to design a feature clock specifically for the barrel vault sixty feet high. Set against its graded blue background, the outcome has held the attention of all, adults and children alike, since its unveiling in January, 1987, by the enigmatic nature of the concept, the quality of the workmanship and the originality of the design.

A duck at the top impossibly lays a constant stream of golden eggs, which pass onto a large millwheel rotating on a planetary gear. Each egg in turn is transferred by the millwheel to the cabinet of the clock, where its arrival disturbs a mouse which briefly pops out of one of the many trap doors in the casing.

Below is suspended the magnificent 'Wishing Fish' which gives the clock its name. Twelve feet long, conceptualised and constructed personally by Kit Williams, the fish is craftsmanship of the highest quality. It turns constantly from side to side to display its elegant curves. On the hour, while other actions take place, the fish comes to life, wagging its tail and fins, blowing large bubbles into the mall below to the accompaniment of appropriate music. If a child catches a bubble, perhaps he or she gets a wish.

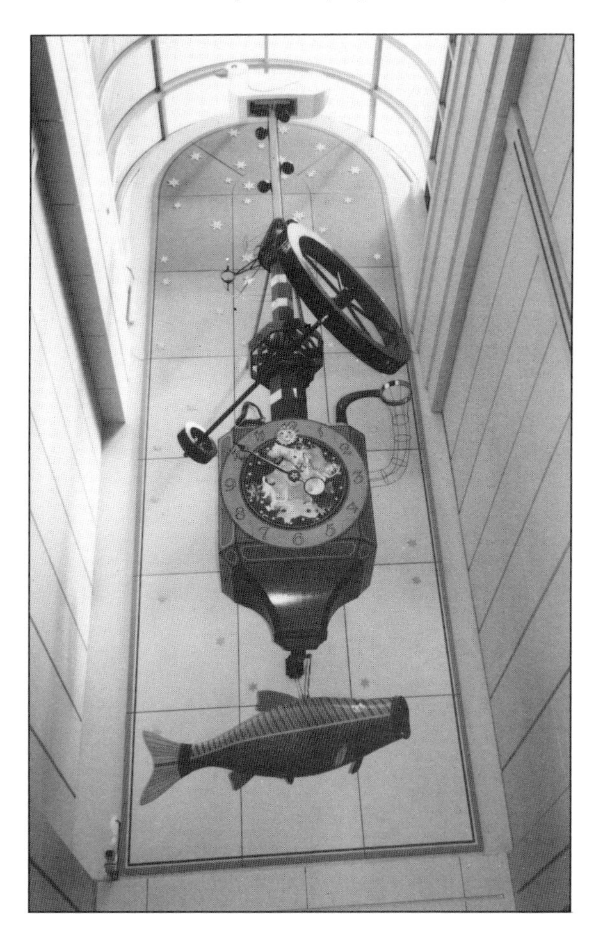

The style and finish of the millwheel and the brassbound mahogany stem of the clock evoke thoughts of Victorian pumproom engineering and the cabinet is finished in the style of an early railway carriage. The working and structural parts of the clock were built by Michael Harding, a world famous local clockmaker, took a year to make, and weighed three tons.

Off the busy main street, five Elephant Murals depict an escape of three elephants in 1934 from Chapman's Travelling Circus, and the havoc they wrought before finding Bloodworth's corn provision merchant's shop, breaking in, and devouring the food.

Amidst the Regency architecture of the Montpellier Quarter are thirty-two elegant classical statues, the Caryatids (three of painted terracotta, which were used as models for the remainder of stone), each in a different posture, sharing the pavement with an original and rare hexagonal post-box, and which lead up the hill to the Montpellier Pump Room (now a bank) with its magnificent rotunda and ceiling.

BADGEWORTH

A FAMOUS BUTTERCUP

Location: West of A46, one mile south-west of Cheltenham. Sheet 163 90201930

Badgeworth does not owe its etymology to badgers but has two special claims to fame. Firstly, it is one of the most ancient parishes in the kingdom, and secondly it contains the smallest nature reserve in the world. Just 346 square yards (290 sq m), the SSSI was designated in the early 1950s because a rare species of the buttercup family is to be found there. The site at Cold Pool, a small depression in impervious Blue Lias clay, fills seasonally with rain water and run-off from adjoining fields to produce the wetland habitat ideal for the Adder's-tongue Spearwort (Ranunculus ophioglossifolius Vill.)

Fully protected under the 1981 Wildlife and Countryside Act, the Spearwort is known at only one other place in Britain, on a common at Wotton-under-Edge, also in Gloucestershire.

There was a time though when the tranquillity of the area was less than now. Industrial competitiveness was more direct. Jealous guardianship of bell-casting comes to light in the rhyme inscribed on a bell in Holy Trinity:

Badgeworth ringers, they were mad
Because Rigbie made me bad;
But Abel Rudhall, you may see
Hath made me better than Rigbie.

Vicious words from an iron tongue. Shurdington, nearby, is different because here its interest is of more recent date. Leading to the driveway of a modern house is a most splendid set of iron gates: ten feet wide and almost as high, the design unique and the craftsmanship of the highest order, they depict knights in armour in attitudes reminiscent of those found on medieval brasses, crests of birds and animals, with a prancing horse as its centrepiece.

UPTON ST LEONARD'S

OLD TECHNOLOGY

Location: Off the B4073, two miles south-east of Gloucester. Sheet 162 86321494

Now a suburb of Gloucester, this former village has lost its rural identity but has preserved two very unusual items.

In the playground of the former school is a large stone pump quite unique to the area. Though now redundant for all practical purposes, it is still capable of being used. This one does not have the usual arm for pumping but is operated by turning a handle which starts revolving a huge wooden fly-wheel with its iron rim, and was so designed to keep the pumping action continuous, even though the operator may have been resting — advanced technology!

Near to the churchyard entrance there is a most unusual sundial, standing on a plinth and topped with an open iron pyramid. This one does not have the common one face, but three, and can be used no matter what the direction of the sun — another advance!

ELMORE

TWO TALENTS, DIFFERENT SETTINGS

Location: West of the A38, two miles west of Gloucester. Sheet 162 76621491

About a mile from the parish boundary lies Elmore Court, home of the Guise family who have held estates in Gloucestershire from the early days of the thirteenth century.

At the entrance to the Court is a magnificent set of iron Baroque gates. They were made by William Edney, the greatest of Bristol's eighteenth-century blacksmiths, in the style of Tijou, with acanthus and hart's-tongue fern motifs, surmounted by the heraldic crest of the Guise family, a swan rising from a ducal coronet. Not detracting from the beauty of the swan, but certainly emphasising further the skill of the blacksmith-artist, is a Green Man of ancient folklore, foliage sprouting from his beard and hair. Was this central decorative piece added for superstitious reasons? Was it the black-smith adopting the former 'mason's licence' from the medieval craftsmen who added Green Men and other symbolic figures from earlier religions into places of Christian worship, presumably as some sort of insurance — 'to get the best of both worlds'? Originally, before 1712, these gates were erected at Rendcomb, the Guise estate in the Cotswolds, but were transferred here early last century.

Sited at the extreme end of the village for some reason no-one seems able to explain, is the church of St. John the Baptist. In its churchyard is one of the finest table-tombs in the county, and several others nearly as good, dating from the seventeenth and eighteenth centuries. The best has particularly fine carving in relief, with a compact plethora covering the total surface, of mourners, Time, Death, and other symbolical and Renaissance details. On others near-by, skeletons, skulls, cherubs and weeping angels abound. Most have stood well the test of time because Painswick stone, suitable for deep undercutting, has been used for the panels, topped by a harder, weather-resistant Minchinhampton stone table.

GLOUCESTER

EYES OPEN IN THE CITY

Location: At the junction of the A38 and A40. Sheet 162 83211878

Gloucester is dominated by its enormous and beautiful cathedral, the seat or *cathedra* of the Bishop since the formation of the diocese in 1541. Before that, for nearly 450 years, it was the church of a Benedictine monastery, tracing its history to 681 when Osric, a prince of Mercia, founded a monastery on the site. However, for most part it dates from 1089 and was planned by King William's dynamic protégé, Serlo, the first Norman abbot, a labour which took him thirty-three years. The result, of this and of later work — the present tower dates from 1450, for example — is a magnificent monument to the glory of God.

The cathedral can claim to be the birthplace of Perpendicular architecture: the south window is the earliest to have been built in that style (c.1335). The glorious east window, with its commemoration of knights who fought at Crecy and Calais, depicting their shields, Christ and the Apostles, and angels, was probably finished by 1350 — no mean achievement given the then widespread effect of the plague. The colours and detail of form are incredibly beautiful, the breadth of vision in the undertaking is awe-inspiring. But then comes something much more domestic: one light is devoted to a youth playing with a bat and ball. It is known as the *golfer window* — surely not golf in 1350, when the earliest date for the game's invention is c.1425? Who is he and what is he doing? Is he hurling — but that is an Irish pastime? Is he playing hockey? Is this a craftsman's joke or a depiction of an actual person? No-one knows.

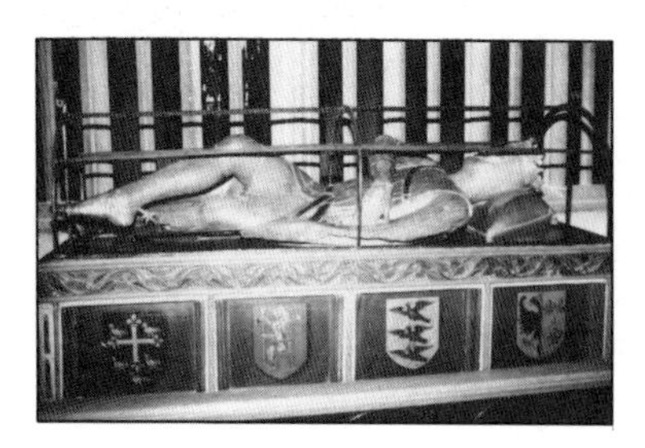

It was here, in an earlier Chapter House than the present, that King William held *deep speech* during the Christmas *Witan* of 1086, following a tradition established by Edward the Confessor of holding a Christmas parliament in Gloucester, and gave orders to begin the audit and survey known to us now as the Domesday Book. It was here where his eldest son was later buried. Robert Courthose aspired to the English throne, but on the Conqueror's death in 1087 was given the Dukedom of Normandy. He distinguished himself on the first crusade but fought his brothers William Rufus and Henry, was eventually captured in 1106 in northern France, and taken to Cardiff Castle where he spent the rest of his life in strict confinement. He died in 1134, and at his own request was buried in the Abbey Church of St. Peter.

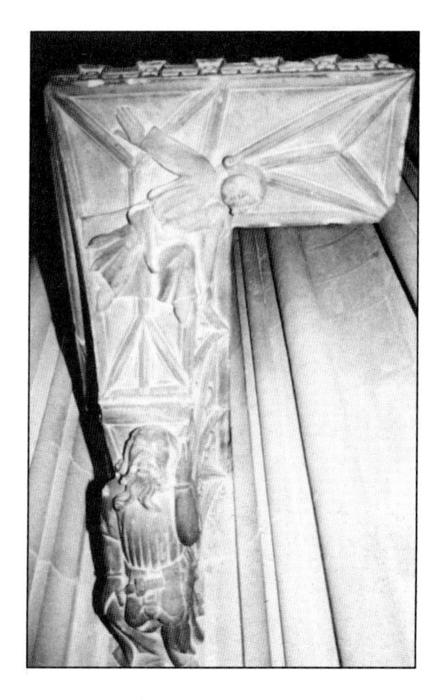

A King of England, Edward II, who was murdered at Berkeley Castle in 1327, rests under one of the most thrilling of all tomb canopies clearly the work of a genius. The boy King Henry III was crowned here but due to the size of his head not with a crown but with his mother's bracelet. Gloucester is one of only four cathedrals in the realm to have witnessed a royal burial and coronation within its walls.

Even here curiosities can be found, among the awesome richness and beauty. The *Prentice Bracket*, an isolated and unique structure, sticks out of the wall in the south transept. It forms a mason's square and may commemorate an apprentice who was killed when he fell from a vault during the building of the cathedral. The monks' choir stalls are perfect, with their three-dimensional ogee-arched canopies and a wonderful series of forty-six misericords dating from the mid-fourteenth century. Rather than the religious subjects one might expect, these carvings consist of folk-tales, domestic scenes and fabulous monsters — two boys playing with a ball, or a huntsman with beater and falcon, for example. One explanation is that the subject was left to the carpenter's imagination, and no-one saw them afterwards except the monks during long services. Of historical interest more than aesthetic, they do give an insight into the medieval mind, in which humour appears to have been coarse rather than keen, and not separate from religious devotion.

The cathedral is particularly rich in monuments, several worthy of particular note. In the north ambulatory is the monument of the last abbot of St. Peter's Abbey, William Parker. The effigy, of c.1535, is of carved alabaster and though he prepared the tomb for himself, after the Dissolution he was not buried here. So who usurped his place? Instead of one mitred abbot, Parker, shown vested in full pontificals, two bishops, a Marian and an Elizabethan, lie below — one a Catholic, one a Protestant. Enough to make Parker shudder.

Two monuments are particularly poignant because they depict infants with their mothers. In the Lady Chapel, Elizabeth Williams rests on her right elbow, her swaddled infant beside her. She died in childbirth in 1622, and was the daughter of Miles Smith, one of the translators of the Authorised Version of the Bible and credited with writing the preface. He was Bishop during the years when William Laud was Dean; as a Puritan he found it extremely difficult to get on with Laud and after a confrontation swore he would never again enter the cathedral so long as Laud remained.

In the north aisle is a monument to Sarah Morley, who died in 1784 at sea in passage from India. Here three angels receive her and her baby from the rolling waves. The sculptor was John Flaxman who was the designer of Wedgewood Pottery medallions and cameos.

In the south aisle, Alderman John Jones, who died in 1630, is shown in a painted half-length upright effigy. This monument by the Southwark workshops, and erected during his lifetime, is full of delightful details such as the packets of deeds in pigeon-holes and dated 1581-1630, for he was registrar to eight bishops; he is shown in mayoral robes for he was three times Mayor of the city; he was also Member of Parliament from 1603–14.

In the precincts of the cathedral, the cloisters have the earliest fan-vaulting known, dating between 1351 and 1377. Though officially a passage communicating with other parts of the monastery, the monks must have dallied from time to time for against the north wall is a stone bench on which are traces of scratchings indicating that the novices played a game called *Nine Men's Morris* or *Fox and Geese.*

There is much of curious interest in the city also. One of the earliest inns to double as a theatre was the New Inn, which like so many 'New Inns' is very old indeed. Built around 1457 to cater for the pilgrims who poured into the city to visit Edward II's tomb, it has retained the flagged court-yard where the players performed at one end and the peasantry watched from the other, in what was called 'the pit', while the more favoured customers looked down from the galleries and windows It has yet another place in national history, for here on 10 July, 1553, the ill-fated Lady Jane Grey was proclaimed Queen of England.

One of the most famous retail establishments is the shop of the *Tailor of Gloucester*. Beatrix Potter's version of the story is familiar and the shop is the same mixture of fact and fantasy. Miss Potter copied its exterior in her book, but her drawings of the interior were based on a local cottage which she had visited. When her enterprising publishers later acquired the tiny shop at 9 College Court, built onto the stone wall of Cathedral Close, they remodelled the interior to her drawings from around Stroud and Harescombe.

One of Gloucester's finest old houses is tucked away behind a garden shop, up a passage only three feet wide. Maverdine House, also called the Judge's House, is a towering four-storey mansion of great opulence and was the headquarters of Cromwell's commander, Colonel Massey, during the siege of the city in the Civil War. He may have found it convenient to have such a narrow approach in case the Royalists came after him as in the late summer of 1643 his handful of professional soldiers and the citizens of the city turned the tide of the Civil War and changed the course of history. Certainly its narrowness has made life difficult for photographers ever since.

On the east side of St. Mary's Square a beautiful monument, with Decorated-style canopy, was erected in 1862 on the site of Bishop Hooper's martyrdom in 1555. In 1551, Hooper had been consecrated Bishop of Gloucester by Edward VI, but his radical attitude nearly wrecked his episcopal career before it began because he chose to be imprisoned rather than consent to wear the traditional vestments at his consecration ceremony. A compromise was eventually reached, he was released from prison, consecrated, and came to Gloucester to redeem his province. He was a serious, dour, conscientious man who gave three or four sermons a day, and was horrified at the laxity of the clergy: some did not know the Ten Commandments or even the Lord's Prayer. In trying to improve the situation, he made many enemies.

However, Bishop Hooper worked unceasingly, never sparing himself, not only in one diocese but two, for he had to look after Worcester as well.

His wife worried because of his overworking and feared he might break down. He probably would have ruined his health but, after two-and-a-half years of his episcopate, King Edward died. His sister, Mary, a devout Catholic, succeeded him: with her accession, the Reformation came to a halt. Because of his Protestant tendencies Hooper became a marked man. Not for nothing did the Queen earn the nickname 'Bloody Mary', as the number of victims she sent to their deaths would signify. Hooper was ordered to London and deprived of his office because of his marriage and his denial of trans-substantiation. He was sent to the harsh Fleetwood prison on an unfounded charge of owing money to the Crown, and spent a year in a vile, stinking chamber where he became infected with disease. Eventually he was sent back to Gloucester for execution, and four days later, on 9 February, at 9am, he was taken to the stake.

News spread quickly. A crowd of about 7,000 gathered to witness the death of this brave man. His ordeal in the flames lasted three-quarters of an hour, and the pyre had to be lit three times. Three bladders of gunpowder which had been strapped to his body exploded but because they were badly positioned poor John Hooper remained conscious. His final moments were described by a witness:

> *. . . but when he was black in the mouth, and his tongue swollen, that he could not speak, yet his lips went till they were shrunk to the gums. He knocked his breast with his hands, until one of his arms fell off. He then knocked with the other, what time the fat, water and blood dropped at his fingers ends, until by renewing of the fire his strength was gone, and his hand did cleave fast in knocking to the iron on his breast. So, immediately bowing forwards, he yielded up his spirit.*

By a strange coincidence, when he was made Bishop he had chosen for his coat-of-arms the lamb in the burning bush. Was this prescience?

There is a small room in the old St. Mary's Gate overlooking the site of his martyrdom. Since the days of Hooper's death, reports have been made of a ghostly face seen gazing from a window. Is this the face of Queen Mary, who was responsible for his fate? It is said that she travelled secretly to Gloucester to ensure the deed was carried out according to her wishes. However, this can only remain speculation since no evidence has been found to substantiate the claim. The face may be just that of a curious onlooker — but nonetheless a witness to that terrible event.

The gate-house with its eighteenth-century wrought-iron work and gilded cherubs opens into the cathedral precincts and, besides the royal spectre, has another claim to fame: it was where the rhyme of Humpty-Dumpty was composed — Humpty being a large vat of tar, which spilled when the gatehouse was being built centuries ago.

There was a time when tradesmen's signs were popular forms of advertising. In Southgate Street is a curious clock dating from 1904 over the premises of a watch-maker and jeweller's shop. The figures of Father time, a Welshman, a Scotsman, John Bull and an Irishwoman are almost life-sized and represent their countries. Father Time strikes the hours and the other figures strike their bells on the quarters. The clock is so designed that the figures strike only between 9am and 9pm.

There are other signs. A giant gilded grasshopper served to advertise a retailer of fine foods and wines. An enormous carved wooden black dog, with bright red tongue, sat on the parapet of the Black Dog Inn. The tradition has not been lost, and ingenious ways are still used to attract the attention of passers-by. A canoeist advertises a sports shop below by impossibly sticking out of a third-floor window, and the world-famous Double Gloucester cheese gives its name to a pub.

Along Southgate, just behind the church of St. Mary de Crypt, in the far left corner of what used to be a graveyard, is a strange-looking tower. A plaque states that *Addison's Folly* was created in honour of Robert Raikes, the founder in 1770 of the National Sunday School movement who lived just across the road and whose first school was in this church. This is the official version: actually, a sad story lies behind its construction.

Thomas Fenn Addison's sister, Catherine, had left her previous home in Homerton, Middlesex, to reside in Gloucester, following her marriage to a local wine merchant, William Washbourne. Thomas followed, became a young attorney and much involved in local affairs. In 1839 Thomas married Hannah Sheldon in Exeter, and the young couple settled in the former home of Robert Raikes in Bell Lane. He was an excellent solicitor and the couple were very happy together. They had a large family of eight children: seven girls and one son. Their happiness was short-lived, however. In 1856, when only forty years old, Hannah died, and was buried in the churchyard at Hempsted.

Six years later the old Crypt School room was sold at auction. The garden at the rear was bought by Thomas Addison for £57. In 1864 he began work on the Tower. There were complaints that it would obstruct the footpath so he promised the town council that as soon as it was completed all would be well: after all, he argued it was a memorial to Robert Raikes. When the Tower was completed a plaque was indeed put onto the building to Raikes's memory: the only problem was that one needed a ladder to read it for it was so small and high up.

Thomas used to climb the tower and look through a telescope at his wife's resting place, an activity from which he derived much comfort. Within a year of the tower being completed, however, poor Thomas passed away. The residence and tower were later sold, when it was described as '*a sort of memorial to Robert Raikes*': in truth it was a memorial to Thomas's love of Hannah.

LLANTHONY

OF MONKS AND THERAPEUTIC WATER

Location: A quarter of a mile south-west of Gloucester. Sheet 162 81551755

The ruins of Llantony Priory lie only a quarter of a mile south-west of Gloucester cathedral: but a Welsh name in a city suburb?

The priory of Llanthony was founded originally c.1109 under the Augustinian rule in the Honddu area of the Black Mountains by a Norman baron. Surrounded by hostile people in their remote valley, the monks were

very much troubled by the marauding Welsh

and begged the Bishop of Hereford to find them a less dangerous place in which to live. The Bishop in turn addressed himself to Milo, Earl of Hereford and Constable of Gloucester, who gave a piece of land south of the city. The monks fled Wales, and built a second Llanthony at Gloucester, which was consecrated in 1136, under the patronage of Milo. To emphasise that the new priory was intended to be no more than a daughter-house, it too was called Llanthony, this time Llanthony Secunda, or Llanthony St. Mary, to distinguish it from Llanthony St. John in Wales. During the following centuries the Gloucester priory received many great endowments and lands in the county and elsewhere; situated as it was under the shadow of Gloucester Castle, it prospered far more than the remote monastery in Wales.

On the steep slope of the hill, a spring bubbles out of the stony hillside and over it the monks of Llanthony Secunda built St. Ann's Well — though probably its origins lie much deeper in our pagan history. Centuries earlier, the Romans had a camp on the hillside behind it and no doubt the water was as sweet then as it is now, while countless generations in between have come here to drink, to wash and to bathe their eyes as the water was believed a cure for eye diseases of all kinds: indeed, many still call it the Holy Well.

BROOKETHORPE

INTERNECINE STRIFE

Location: On the A 4173, three miles south of Gloucester. Sheet 162 83501237

In 1644, Royalists and Parliamentarians fought a pitched battle on Huddiknoll Hill. The latter were forced to retreat down a steep and narrow lane towards Brookethorpe and the slaughter was considerable. In 1855, skeletons and helmets were found — some local folk using the helmets for coal-scuttles.

At the end of the Civil War, though, feelings continued to run high, dividing villages and even families. On the wood cornice of the porch of the ancient church of St. Swithin one parishioner made a rudely carved chronogram, with all the 'Ns' in reverse writing, commemorating the execution of Charles I:

Ter Deno IanI Labens reX soLe Co dente CaroLUs eXUtUs soLio sCeptroqUe ser Cure.

When the letters in upper case are translated into Roman numerals, they add up to 1648, the fateful year in which Charles lost his throne, sceptre and head.

How was such an ingenious inscription devised in this quiet backwater, and carved by some unskilled hand? The author-carver was literate and numerate, educated in Latin. Clearly it was put in this place to be highly visible, for all to see, but by whom, to whom? Was the Vicar responsible for it? Was carving in the woodwork of the church a local past-time? The porch is covered with graffiti of considerable age — 1670, 1676, and so on.

A mile south of Brookethorpe a curiously-named hamlet has virtually disappeared but preserves its title: Bacchus. Why was this quiet, almost insignificant spot named after the Roman god of wine? Does it signify some well-deserved reputation of former residents' propensity for bacchanalian feats?

SAUL

ORNAMENTAL FRIENDS

Location: Six miles south-west of Gloucester, west of A38. Sheet 162 74800950

The ornament of a house is the friends who frequent it,

wrote Emerson. Others of us are not so fortunate as to have ornamental friends but still like to display something more tangible to make our house different from the rest, something which allows even our most modest dwelling become distinctive and unique.

The village of Saul marks the place where the Stroudwater Canal crosses the Gloucester-Berkeley Canal, where the public house is called The Junction Inn to recognise this fact — and is a typical nineteenth-century canal pub — and where many of the houses, again nearly all early to mid-nineteenth-century, declare their allegiance to the trades of their former occupants. Facing the church of St. James, a house dated 1829 has a carved lion on the sill, and next to Victoria Place is a cottage dated 1858 boldly presenting the carved figures of twin sailors and a pair of doves. Opposite that, a cottage of 1802 has under a gable a carving of the bust of just one sailor. All are painted in bright contemporary colours, and add to the gaiety of the village without a trace of garishness.

Perhaps though the most curious logo is that on a gate in the main street which presumably serves as a caveat to the local dogs — or is it to their owners?

FRAMPTON-ON-SEVERN

GREEN AND ORANGE

Location: West of A38, eight miles south-west of Gloucester. Sheet 162 75550755

Frampton-on-Severn has lost the main ingredient that gave it its name. Though within sight of the Severn, the river can now only be reached by crossing a canal and at least three fields. But it has other compensations. The village green is wide, long and flat, a vast expanse of lush meadow some 750 yards long and 130 yards wide at its broadest. At twenty-two acres it is England's largest, with three ponds dignified by swans, and a cricket ground. It is often called Rosamund's Green, recalling the mysterious Jane Clifford, Henry II's 'Fair Rosamund'.

A most outstanding house on the Green, the Palladian-style Frampton Court, was built between 1731 and 1733 for Richard Clutterbuck, an official of the Bristol Customs House. It was here the original water-colours of the *Frampton Flora* were discovered. A rectangular ornamental canal to the north-west of the house is terminated by a stunning virtuoso display of Gothick, one of the finest garden pavilions in Britain. The designer of this mid-eighteenth-century Orangery is not known, though it may well have been William Halfpenny and his son, John, who together published in 1752 *Chinese and Gothic Architecture Properly Ornamented.*

The Orangery has been adapted superbly to a holiday-let, and is available via the Estate office.

Across the Green, at Old Manor Farm, is a tall, octagonal seventeenth-century dovecote, and an even older barn.

Frampton-on-Severn prospered when the Gloucester-Berkeley Ship Canal opened in 1827. At Splatt Bridge is one of the canal-keeper's houses, which look like Greek temples and were designed by the architects of the canal, Telford and Mylne.

EASTINGTON

A SUPERB BUILDING AND A GUIDING HAND

Location: East of A38, nine miles south of Gloucester. Sheet 162 77390548

At the end of the village, presiding over the garden of Alkerton Grange, is a unique early Georgian gazebo of richly-coloured brick. This unexpected delight has an imposing facade with stone dressings, and an open segmental pediment with three splendid urns, one borne on the head of a satyr.

But who designed it and what is it doing here? The architect is not known, nor precisely the date, and local tradition holds that this garden house was brought from elsewhere. Doubtful that may be, but there is no evidence for it being part of a water garden, even though its design and form, tall and rather narrow, up a short flight of steps, seem to require a canal in front to reflect its image. Conjecturally, it may be related to similar structures at Westbury and Frampton, both of which show evidence of Dutch influence, but there is no documentation to help us. Even so, our enjoyment of its beauty is not lessened.

When travelling through Eastington, look out for the finger-post at the junction of roads in the centre of the village, for it is a most unusual example. A tall pillar in the centre of the road system, it has ornate iron arms under stone gables, topped by an elaborate carved finial. You may find the directions difficult to read but the arms are at exactly the right height for stage-coach drivers.

FROCESTER

A MAGNIFICENT TITHE BARN

Location: Nine miles south of Gloucester, east of A38. Sheet 162 78620298

Frocester Court occupies the site of the manor house and desmesne farm of the monastic estate granted by Ravenswart, brother of King Beornwulf of Mercia, in 823 to the monks of Gloucester, who held it almost without break until the dissolution in 1539. The timber-framed section of the Gatehouse is traditionally thought to have been erected to commemorate the visit by Elizabeth I in 1574 on her way to Berkeley Castle. However, the attractive timberwork is a late Victorian restorative facade of c.1900, covering earlier simpler framing. Even so, it is a wonderful structure.

The massive barn is one of the largest and certainly one of the best preserved in England, still used as intended, very much a necessary part of the busy farm, and substantially as built originally. Of local oolitic limestone, it is 186 feet long, 30 feet wide, 12 feet to the eaves and 36 feet to the ridge. Inside, one is struck by the appearance of the massive oak roof timbers, originally held together by oak pegs. What vast tracts of land did the Benedictine monastery cover to fill this superb collecting house with tithes?

How good at his fractions was the old abbot John de Gamages, who had caused a *Great Barn of Froucester* to be built between 1284 and 1306, for many, many thousands of tenths would have been needed to warrant such an edifice. Whatever his counting system, the net result is still an enrichment of the landscape.

Within the farm complex, other buildings, though adapted to modern usages, are historically important. The attractive arch-fronted block in front of the barn are mid-nineteenth-century cowsheds, and other buildings are substantially older, mentioned in an inventory of 1628, including a stable, sheep pen and pigeon house.

SHARPNESS

CURIOUS NAMES AND A CURIOUS BUILDING

Location: On the B4066, fifteen miles south-west of Gloucester. Sheet 162 67000300

Sharpness marks the entrance to the canal which was opened in 1827, after thirty-three years of digging, in order to provide a permanent passage to Gloucester docks and overcome the vagaries of the tidal Severn. At low tide can still be seen the hulks of a dozen or so Severn trows, the sailboats which used to ply the river, but are used no longer.

The flat plain north and east is a fascinating area, full of curiosities. Village names alone are interesting. The village of Purton, upstream from Sharpness, is on the east bank of the Severn, but the hamlet of Purton is exactly opposite on the other side. This is no ordinary division of a village: to visit one Purton from the other, it is necessary to make a journey of at least thirty miles. This also is where the spectacular Severn Bore begins to gather itself for its surge upriver.

Breadstone is an unusual combination of words to form a name, and has a most curious church. St. Michael's is not on raised ground like the majority with similar dedications, and is built entirely of tin: its roof and walls are corrugated, and the attempt at a tiny spire looks as if it has been cut rather clumsily from a large can with a giant tin-opener. Amazingly, the entire exterior has been painted blue! Inside is different: the walls are lined with wood, and a small, round east window in modern style casts a warm glow everywhere.

This village is surrounded by unusual names: Tumpy Green is a mile to the north, Leathern Bottle lies to the east, and Wanswell to the west. The latter stands on the site of the former Saxon Berkeley Abbey and derives its name from a pagan dedication of its well to Woden (Odin), father of Thor, who was the principal Teutonic god, the Norse god of war, learning and poetry; he is still commemorated in our Wednesday. Such a name indicates both the well's antiquity and the reluctance of locals to christianise — and in their eyes possibly to dilute the fertility-giving power of — the deity who, according to older religions, dwelt in it.

BERKELEY

THE FOLLIES OF POWER

Location: Sixteen miles south-west of Gloucester, of the B4066. Sheet 162 68509900

Berkeley's towers appear in martial pride
Menacing all around the champaign wide
Right famous as the seat of barons bold
And valiant earls whose great exploits are told.
Michael Drayton

Berkeley is dominated by the Castle. It began as a fortress in 1117 but was gradually enlarged and adapted over several centuries. As this process of 'modernisation' ceased for all practical purposes as long ago as the reign of Edward III in the fourteenth century, when domestic architecture was still in a rude and inelegant state, there are few sumptuous galleries. Instead the visitor will find narrow passages, twisting staircases and doorways which could be held against attack by a few men armed with sword and pike — and the room where Edward II was murdered in 1327.

It is though the outside which is, for us, the most fascinating part. Built on an eminence for security reasons, the peculiar colour of its walls are unique: rose-pink supplied by square blocks of sandstone from the banks of the neighbouring Severn, and iron-grey from sandwich-thin slabs of tufa, a porous calcareous stone resembling pumice. Especially at sunset, the Castle turns almost purple and it is hard to realise that it is a man-made stronghold. The stronghold theme is continued in more recent buildings, giving them the qualities of follies. Within the Castle grounds, the explorer may be puzzled by what is apparently an eighteenth-century country house standing at a little distance amongst the trees. Park House is a castellated eye-catcher, almost black-and-white, the pale random stone violently fortified with very dark dressing early in the nineteenth century. Here the kennels and offices of the world-famous Hunt are alive with the voices of hounds.

Though later in date, Park Lodges are in much the same style, and on the B4066 is a castellated cottage.

BERKELEY

SCIENTIFIC EXPERIMENTS LEAD TO GLOBAL GRATITUDE

Within the Castle's shadow, of humbler proportions but of world-wide importance, is the little *Temple of Vaccinia.* Hardly a root hut, though said to have been designed by Thomas Wright, it is no more than a rustic thatched garden shed with bark plastered on its brick walls, and an ingenious fireplace; this is where Edward Jenner vaccinated his first patients, the local poor free of charge.

Jenner was born in 1749, the youngest son of the Vicar of Berkeley. He began his medical studies at the age of fourteen apprenticed to a surgeon in Sodbury, and later went to London to study under Hunter, the great anatomist, at St. George's Hospital. He was twenty-three when, a successful medical man, he returned to his native Berkeley and settled into life as a country doctor while pursuing his interests in natural history and music. Over the next twenty-five years he made detailed observations of local birds and mammals, pioneering studies into the hibernation of hedgehogs and the life cycle of the cuckoo, performed various scientific experiments, especially those in attempting to launch a hydrogen balloon, wrote medical papers and tended his patients.

For centuries, smallpox had been the greatest killer of mankind. It has been estimated that it caused the deaths of some sixty million victims in the seventeenth century alone. Jenner knew of the belief of country people, no more than folklore, that those who caught cowpox, a mild disease, would never catch smallpox. To test this belief, he reasoned that if he could transmit cowpox from person to person, he could protect them from smallpox. Finally, in 1796, Dr Jenner vaccinated a local boy, James Phipps, with cowpox taken from a milkmaid, Sarah Nelms, who in turn had caught it from her Red Gloucester cow, Blossom. A month later he infected him with active smallpox. Nothing untoward happened. Jenner had shown that the boy was now immune to smallpox. The science of immunology was born. The local lad who trustingly submitted himself to Jenner's experimental vaccinations was rewarded by the grateful doctor with a cottage for life. On an international scale, the eradication of the disease had begun: in 1980 the World Health Organisation announced that the process had been completed.

BERKELEY

THE VENOM OF GOSSIP REVISITED

Every opportunity was taken for a church to be a 'teaching aid', to reinforce visually the preachings of Vicar — 'Dooms' and other wall paintings were used, as here at St. Mary's, and carver-masons too played their part in conveying a moral didactic intent. On a capital of the nave is a thirteenth-century sermon in stone, a corbel depicting two female gossips with a toad sitting on their heads. Was this to teach that gossip is like the venom of a toad? Was it to reinforce the local legend that a gigantic toad, so evil and venomous, was kept in the Castle dungeon and fed on hapless prisoners thrown in there? Was it a medieval warning against false rumour? Did the sculptor have anyone particular in mind as models — if the cap fits, wear it?

In the churchyard are two tombs which the curiosity explorer must seek out. The Horologist's Tomb, a noble altar tomb of 1685, is to a watchmaker, aged 77, and throws some unexpected light on the activities of that craft three centuries ago:

Here lyeth Thomas Peirce, who no man taught.
Yet he in Iron, Brass and Silver wrought.
He Jacks, and Clocks and Watches (with art) made
And mended too when others works did fade.
Of Berkeley, five times Mayor this Artist was
And yet this Mayor, this Artist is but grass.
And when his own Watch ran Downe on the last Day
He that made up Watches, has not made the Key
To winde it Up, but Useless it must lie
Until he Rise Againe no more to die.

In another table-tomb lies a man of a different profession. Dicky Pearce, who died in 1728, was England's last court jester, and his epitaph is said to have been written by Dean Jonathon Swift, author of *Gulliver's Travels*:

Here lies the Earl of Suffolk's fool,
Men called him Dicky Pearce,
His folly served to make folks laugh
When wit and mirth were scarce.
Poor Dick alas is dead and gone
What signifies to cry?
Dickys enough are still to come
To laugh at by and by.

TORTWORTH

A GNARLED GIANT AND OTHERS

Location: Three miles west of Wotton-under-Edge, off the B4509.	Sheet 162 70509340

A gnarled giant lives minutes away from Junction 14 of the M5.

A tree can become as much an object of interest and pilgrimage as any other monument: the fact that it is living gives it appeal; that it is ancient makes it a special claimant. The Tortworth Chestnut is so old that it is marked on the Ordnance Survey as an historic monument. Indeed, a plaque beside this sweet or Spanish chestnut (*castanea sativa*) dates it as 600 years old in 1800. Not surprisingly, it has gathered such legends that it is now difficult to distinguish myth from reality.

Some say the tree may have been planted by the Romans, who introduced the species to England, using the chestnuts to make bread for the (common) soldiers. Certainly it was a "notable tree" in the time of King Stephen, c.1135, and as a chestnut tree takes 250 years to reach maturity, its age can be worked out. In his *History of Gloucestershire* of 1712, Sir Robert Atkyns confirms it as already an antiquity:

> *There is a remarkable chestnut growing in the garden belonging to the Manor House, which by tradition is said to have been growing there in the reign of King John. It is 19 yards in compass . . .*

A local *Flora* by Witchell and Strugnell, published in Stroud in 1892, gave the tree's measurements as forty-nine feet in girth, with its branches covering a circle of thirty-two yards, about one-sixth of an acre, making it a small copse in itself.

The species of sweet chestnut has a reputation for longevity, but clearly this particular example has found the soil and climate of Tortworth to its liking. Though the centre is an old, worn butt, "a decaying mass of wood" even a hundred years ago, a number of sizeable, healthy trees are growing on each side, leaning away from the main pollarded trunk: it will be alive for a long time yet. In the field beside the church, it looks more like an ancient copse than a single tree, its twisted limbs spreading along the ground.

This is not the only tree here which will fascinate aborealists. In a field over the churchyard wall is the actual Tulip Tree mentioned in the *Observer's Book of Trees*, an American Hickory which still bears nuts (American frontiersmen lined their jerkins with them as protection against Indian arrows, and their wives ground them for flour); a Silver-leafed Lime or Linden, with a branch span of 106 feet, one of the largest in England and remarkable for its almost perfect symmetry; a Cedar of Lebanon (the species whose wood was used extensively in the construction of King Solomon's Temple, and the oil of which was used in ancient Egypt to embalm the dead); and two Locust Trees, the fruit of which is supposed to have provided John the Baptist with his "locusts and wild honey" and whose wood was used to make the pegs which fastened together the timbers of battleships at Trafalgar.

The arboreal connection in the area continues. Tradition has it that Walter Raleigh did his early courting of Bess Throckmorton here: after all, they called their first son (conceived out of wedlock) Damerie, and Damery is the name of a quiet wooded hamlet just down the road.

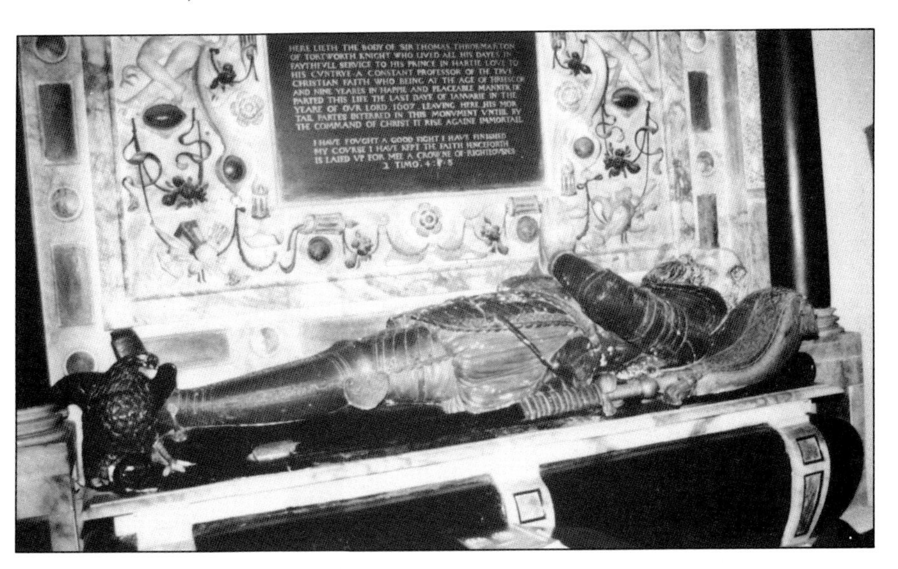

THORNBURY

ANYTHING YOU CAN DO, I CAN DO BETTER

Location: Nine miles north of Bristol, on B4061, west of A38. Sheet 172 63949050

Thornbury is best known for its early-sixteenth-century castle — though it was intended to be more of a palace within — begun by Edward Stafford, 3rd Duke of Buckingham, and only partially completed when he was executed in 1521. For 200 years it remained uninhabited, but in 1720 was partly roofed and in 1811 Lord Henry Howard restored portions though the whole was not finally completed until 1854.

Despite this political inactivity, commercial prosperity ensured Thornbury's steady growth. Particularly important was the coaching trade, and inns competed for custom by advertising their services in the usual way — by visual display. Still standing opposite each other in the High Street, the eighteenth-century White Lion is distinguished by a splendid painted cast lion over the portico, while across the road on the Swan Hotel sits a more sedate bird. Both creatures are enormous and no doubt grew in size to compete for the attention of travellers and coach-drivers. Neither proprietor was going to be outdone.

COMPTON GREENFIELD

HOLLYWOOD PARK TOWER

Location: West of the M5, three miles north of Bristol. Sheet 172 57288121

From the M5, to the west of Junction 17, can be seen the Hollywood Park Tower. Built of local ashlar, the tall tower is square with chamfered corners, its parapet battlemented, and with a taller stair turret. It has two storeys and three bays with semi-circular recesses ornamented with draped spears over the ground-floor windows, and a semi-circular Roman Doric portico. The contemporary interior fittings have Regency motifs.

Buttressed at the base and with a relatively small clock-face, it resembles a church tower without a church. It was built for Sir John Davis some time between 1848 and 1854, and although the architect's original drawings still exist, they are not signed, unfortunately. Possibly the Tower was the work of Francis Niblett, the church architect, who was active in this area at that time.

Davis had purchased the estate, then called Holly Hill, in 1839, but did not retire there from the Governorship of Hong Kong until 1848. It is not known if he won or was given the clock but in either case he had to build a tower to put it in.

In the early days of aviation the Tower was used by the Whites as a landmark to fly around, and when the flag was being lowered even the Graf Zeppelin dipped its nose in salute as it cruised by. Curious buildings seem to grow in the area, for the gatehouse at nearby Over Court has sitting on its top a large obelisk, in rich local limestone, with carved lyre-end buttresses. Not only buildings but roads, too: at Almondsbury is the unusually named 'Sundays Hill'.

IRON ACTON

THE KNIGHT ON THE TOWER

Location: On the B4058, six miles north-west of Bristol. Sheet 172 68038352

The name of this village derives from tun, township, timbered with *ac*, or oak, where iron ore is dug. Not every person passing through will notice the figure on the tower of St. James the Less.

Looking over the top is a knight in armour, his hands folded in the attitude of prayer. Now much weathered, he sits on a bracket and is waist-length high above the parapet. But who is he? What is he doing here? This is not an effigy from a tomb but looks as if it was made for this position. Is he a knight looking over his lands? What clues have we?

From very soon after the Conquest, the family of Acton had held the manor, descending through several generations to Sir John Acton who died without issue in 1344. His estates passed to his heiress, his cousin Maud (or Matilda), who had already become the second wife of Sir Nicholas Poyntz of Cory Mallet. By then Sir Nicholas had already been dead for several years and Maud was an elderly woman. On her death the estates passed to her son, Sir John.

Inside the church is a recumbent effigy in armour of the same style as the figure on the parapet. It is likely that this unidentified person was Sir John Poyntz, who died in 1376. There are also three incised slabs on the church floor: these represent Robert Poyntz and his two wives, Anne and Katherine, identified by the tomb inscription:

> *Here lyeth Robert Poyntz Lord of Iren Acton and thys stepyl here maked, who deyde the fyftene day of Junne, the year of oure Lord MCCCCXX of whos sowle God have mercy. Amen.*

Robert, who actually died in 1439, was the son of John. While it is not possible to identify definitively the knight on the tower, a plausible explanation is that when Robert *this stepyl here maked* (1439) he put up the effigy to commemorate his father, just as the churchyard cross is believed from the arms on it to commemorate his wife and his Acton grandmother.

There are other interesting features in this church. The richly carved Jacobean pulpit has retained its almost perfect canopy, and is inscribed:

> *Robert Hoopper Parson; Thomas Leg and Mighill Tuck, Churchwardins Anno 1624*

There is also a stone font of unusual design, uniquely incorporating a book-rest carved onto its rim, presumably so the Vicar can give all his attention to the child without having to hold his Baptismal book simultaneously.

The dominant feature of the churchyard is the large cross. This is early-fifteenth-century, square, standing on a base of three octagonal steps. The upper stage has two shields on each face, each held by an angel with long drooping wings, four charged with the symbols of the Passion, two blank, and two bearing the arms of Acton and Acton impaling FitzNicoll. Robert Poyntz's second wife was Katherine FitzNicoll and his grandmother was Maud Acton: as he does not use his own paternal arms it must be supposed that he had for the time, as was his right, used the arms of his grandmother. He died in 1439 so the date of the Cross must be a little earlier. The Cross on the top has disappeared. In 1875 Rimmer wrote:

> *. . . the stone of which it is made is very hard and the carvings on it are perfect; but it has been mutilated designedly. It has evidently been destroyed by heavy missiles, there are marks on the upper part where stones have struck but whether the remaining part was too solid for mischief or whether the inhabitants of the houses on either side objected to the proceedings, we are not informed.*

HENBURY

A SLAVE LIES HERE

Location: Two miles north-west of Bristol, east of M5. Sheet 172 56407880

In the eighteenth century, much of Bristol's wealth derived from the slave trade. Whilst slaves were not common in the city some merchants and members of the aristocracy did keep them, more for their curiosity value than anything else, and advertisements in local papers of the time record the offering of rewards for the recapture of runaways.

In the churchyard of St. Mary's is the grave of Scipio Africanus, who died in 1720. The headstone was erected by the Earl of Suffolk in memory of his eighteen-years-old black servant, a freed slave. The carved cherubim are black and the inscription, telling us a good deal more about the master than about the former slave, reads

HERE
Lieth the Body of
SCIPIO AFRICANUS
Negro Servant to ye Right
Honourable Charles William
Earl of Suffolk and Bradon
who died ye 21 December
1720, Aged 18 years.

Unusually, there is a footstone as large as the headstone to Scipio's grave. It too carries a carving of a black cherub and is inscribed with a poem:

I who was born a PAGAN and a SLAVE
Now Sweetly Sleep a CHRISTIAN In my Grave
What tho' my hue was dark my Savior's sight
Shall Change this darkness into radiant light
Such grace to me my Lord on earth has given
To recommend me to my Lord in heaven
Whose glorious second coming here I wait
With saints and Angels Him to celebrate.

If he suffered this snobbish attitude in death, what slights did Scipio have to tolerate in life?

BLAISE HAMLET

NOWHERE A MORE PICTURESQUE PLACE TO LIVE

Location: Off the B4057, four miles north of central Bristol. Sheet 172 55917890

A short way off the M5 in Henbury lies Blaise Hamlet, the finest example in the country of buildings of the Picturesque Movement. To say the least, it is an unusual place, a collection of nine remarkable cottages, each different, making a most delightfully informal arrangement around The Green. This picturesque yet eminently practical model village was designed in 1809 by John Nash and built a year later for the retired and elderly estate workers and labourers of a Quaker owner of the Blaise Estate, the banker John Scandrett Harford.

The elaborate pump on The Green, with its gilded weather vane and pierced *H*, was given as the inscription tells us, in *filial devotion* by Harford's son. There was already a folly on the estate, a triangular castle on the hilltop built in 1766 for a previous owner, Thomas Farr, by Robert Mylne, at a cost of £3,000. It differs from the standard triangular folly-towers in having a circular core with three slightly taller round turrets on the corners.

It is not only professional architects and their wealthy clients who built follies. In November, 1819, the Common Council of Bristol decided to repair and beautify St. Mark's Chapel. Three years later, the very good late-Decorated west window was taken down and a copy put in its place. The old window was given to Mr Cave, a member of the Council, who used it to make a screen in his garden. The window is set between two very amateur towers of rubble, one being slightly taller and capped with a little steeple and weather vane, and the other having a flagstaff. Beside the lower tower is a wall pierced with a tall Gothic arch. This is a most touching amateur folly-work.

HIGHNAM

PATRIARCHAL DEVOTION

Location: Off the B4215, three miles west of Gloucester. Sheet 162 79621960

Here a man and a building are inextricably linked: to understand the unique circumstances that led to the construction of this church it is necessary to understand the man who conceived the whole idea.

In 1837, Highnam estate with 1100 acres, a wharf, mill and woodlands, was purchased by Thomas Gambier Parry, while still only twenty-one years of age. Both his parents had died before his fifth birthday but his father and grandfather had been directors of the East India Company, and great wealth awaited his coming of age. His first thoughts were for a country estate to set down roots that had been lacking in his parentless childhood and youth.

After the early death in 1848 of his wife Isabella, Parry, now a widower at only thirty-two, embarked on the project to build the church and school as a memorial to her and to the several children they had lost in infancy, naming it the Church of the Holy Innocents: an unusual dedication to the children slaughtered by Herod but clearly with his own dead children in mind. Isabella's bust can be found in the side chapel, having been placed there by Parry himself, alone, on the night before the consecration on 29 April, 1851.

The church has been called "the most important Anglican example of painted internal polychromy". Certainly it is a notable monument to the Oxford Movement, for which Parry had engaged as architect a former school friend, Henry Woodyear.

Being set back from the road, surrounded by fields and trees, the Neo-Gothic church is a delight, like stepping in to a jewel-box, with its frescoes and wall-paintings almost as fresh as when Parry painted them himself in 'Spirit fresco', the technique he had invented for use in the English climate. Its slender spire, a copy of that at Salisbury Cathedral is, at 200 feet, a landmark for many miles around. The magnificent rood wall painting, the figures with golden haloes in low relief, is lit only by a single dormer either side. The walls are painted to simulate hanging drapery.

CHURCHAM

A ZULU WAR HERO

Location: Between A40 and A48, three miles west of Gloucester.	Sheet 162 76901838

Be not afraid of greatness:
some men are born great, some achieve greatness,
some have greatness thrust upon them.
Twelfth Night, Act 2, scene 5.

Alfred Henry Hook was born in Churcham of humble circumstances. Now he lies in the churchyard of St. Andrew's under a white marble cross which has a VC carved in the middle of a wreath. He is remembered as one of that gallant band of 153 scarlet-coated British soldiers mainly of the Second Battalion of the 24th Foot, which later became the South Wales Borderers, who on 22–23 January, 1879, fought against 4,000 Zulus at Rorke's Drift, the Swedish Lutheran Mission Station. Such was the level of heroism *above and beyond the call of duty* in what has been called *the bravest stand in British military history*, that eleven VCs were awarded in all, the most ever for any single action.

Hook, through hard work and devotion to duty, had achieved the rank of corporal, and was working in the hospital when the Zulus attacked the camp. His great heroism kept the enemy at bay and saved eight patients. His memorial was erected by 'admiring civilians' and military colleagues, and the inscription is taken, aptly, from 1 Macc. IX, 10.

When you have found the grave, let your eyes wander upwards. St. Andrew's has a most curious spire: its flat sides are shaped like enormous lozenges, covered by wood shingles, and from the ground it doesn't even look symmetrical does it?

Nearby, alongside the railway, is a public house called, in hope, the *Silent Whistle*: was the station-master over-zealous with his noisy signals to engine-drivers?

RUDFORD

A COMMUNAL GRAVE SO FAR FROM HOME

Location: On the B4215, four miles north-west of Gloucester. Sheet 162 77812143

Visitors drive through Rudford without realising it is here. It was not always so, for three-and-a-half centuries ago a terrible event took place.

In the latter part of the eighteenth century when the canal was being excavated through the Leadon valley, a number of bodies were discovered. No explanation could be given other than that they were assumed to be those of men who had fallen in some of the many skirmishes which took place in the neighbourhood during the Civil War. Then in the Spring of 1868 at Barber's Bridge, workmen removing a hillock for the purpose of filling in a pool at its base found a further eighty-six skeletons, which were re-interred in one grave on the spot. What carnage had happened in this quiet, out-of-the-way place?

Lord Herbert's Welsh Army had come to besiege Gloucester for the King but in the retreat on 16 March, 1643, a party of these men met Sir William's force and in the skirmish at 'Barberous Bridge' many died, giving the brook, stained by their blood, its name — *Red Brook*. The skeletons are the remains of these men.

Still other skeletons have been found in the churchyard and under the chancel of St. Mary's church nearby: these were the remains of the dead of Waller's force, who being part of the victorious army were accorded burial in consecrated ground.

The communal grave of those brave Welshmen who met their death in the Royalist cause and had to retreat from Highnam in March, 1643, is marked by an obelisk raised in the nineteenth century, twenty feet high, built from stone taken from the ancient city walls of Gloucester, and which stands high on the bank by the side of the road.

WESTBURY-ON-SEVERN

OF WATER AND A MEDIEVAL MISTAKE

Location: On the A48, nine miles west of Gloucester. Sheet 162 71831382

This village is best known for its garden but has many other features which the curiosity-seeker should not miss. The small but handsomely appointed walled garden, a superb example of the Dutch-style layout from the reign of William of Orange, remains a formal haven of tranquil canals, mown lawns, neat hedges, white-painted benches and fruits espaliered against mellow brick. The garden has ornate topiary and a geometric parterre characteristic of garden planning before the informal layouts of landscape gardeners like Launcelot 'Capability' Brown and Humphrey Repton became accepted fashion. Though little seems to have ruffled the scene for 300 years, it was at one time in an advanced state of dereliction. The straight canal has a pavilion at one end and at the other are wrought-iron clairvoyees, giving framed views of the countryside, flanked by pillars with original pineapple finials.

Do not, though, miss the church of SS. Peter, Paul and Mary. The detached tower is about fifty yards away from the church and was built c.1270 as a garrison or watch-tower, commanding views over the river and country side. It was not until the fourteenth century that the stumpy broached spire was added: made entirely of wood, it is 160 feet high and octagonal, framed on a web of ancient oak beams from the Forest of Dean, and covered completely with 35,000 wood shingles held in place by 100,000 copper nails. The church itself is later, of c.1300. This does not explain though the very curious error in the south aisle window, which has the extraordinary inscription: *This church, built AD 1530, was dedicated to the Virgin Mary.* Clearly a misunderstanding, or the artist was drunk at the time. This is not the only mistake. The designer of a memorial in the chancel was clearly not sure where Asia was for he put it on the globe in the region of Australia!

NEWNHAM

A VISUAL FABLE

Location: On the A48, ten miles south-west of Gloucester. Sheet 162 69101150

Newnham has not always been the quiet village on the west bank of the Severn that it now is; indeed it was once one of the five Great Boroughs of Gloucester, and the chief town west of the Severn. Since early times a settlement seems to have existed here, and by Roman times it was a port of some importance, used for trade up and down the river in coal, bark, wood and charcoal brought down the ancient ways from the Forest of Dean.

Newnham reached its zenith in the early nineteenth century, when in 1807 a quay was built with a twenty foot wall as a mooring for the ships. Cranes and warehouses sprang up to take advantage of the increasing trade promised by the fast-growing railway system. The old tramway tunnel under Haie Hill was converted and became the first railway tunnel in the world in 1809. With the construction of the Sharpness Canal, Newnham's trade was over. The last barge, aptly named *Finis*, left the dock in 1928. Now there is no ferry, no railway, no sands.

Newnham was on the main coach route to the west and many of its public houses remain. One has an historical curiosity built into it. The Victoria Hotel, though dating mainly from the early eighteenth century, has in the staircase window a small panel of glass dated 1622 which illustrates the fable of the grasshopper and the ant. This one is actually a replica, as amazingly the original was stolen from its frame some time ago.

Many churchyards in this part of Gloucestershire have headstones carved in the local speciality of multiple cherubim, but at St. Peter's this stylistic tradition is taken to its limit: one stone has on it a total of thirteen cherubs' heads. Unlucky for some?

The name of the hotel at Broadoak is not consistent with the nautical theme in its car park. Amongst its features, the White Hart sports a small light-house built on the bow of a boat complete with rudder.

NEWENT

OF MARKETS AND WINDMILLS

Location: On the B4215, nine miles north-west of Gloucester. Sheet 162 72402590

Newent, whose name appears in the Domesday record as *Noent*, was the capital town of the old area of Ryelands, which developed its own distinctive breed of sheep. In its dog-legged main street many of its beautiful timber-framed buildings date from Elizabethan times, though the attractive Market Hall was later, built at sometime between 1649 and 1668. It is now a restored timber building with one large room approached by outside stairs, and supported about ten feet above ground level on twelve posts. Cromwell quartered his troops here — presumably the men and horses below and the officers above in the room which is a beautiful example of the architecture of those times. In the 1800s the hall was enclosed at the bottom and here the fire engine was kept, the horses grazing in a nearby orchard. When the alarm was sounded the horses had to be caught, harnessed to the fire engine and galloped to the scene of the incident. Records show that on one occasion a horse dropped dead *en route* — which could not have augured well for the building then on fire.

One set of curious buildings are more modern. An employment park on the site of the old cattle market comprises a collection of offices, all hexagonal and looking as if they are from a moonscape rather than a small town in Gloucestershire.

There are other curiosities to seek out. The church of St. Mary the Virgin has the eleventh-century 'Newent Stone', discovered in 1912 during excavations for a new vestry, and at Castle Hill Farm is a working windmill, which for those brave enough to climb to the top affords breathtaking views of Malvern to the east and the Welsh hills to the west.

Three miles south-west of Newent lies May Hill, which rises to over 900 feet and is a site of attention at the Spring Solstice. Its top knot of trees make it the most distinctive of landmarks: these conifers were planted to commemorate the Golden Jubilee of Queen Victoria. On a clear day it is claimed that from the top you can see as far as the Bristol Channel.

KEMPLEY

A FORTUNATE VILLAGE INDEED

Location: Five miles north-west of Newent, west of the B4215. Sheet 149 67483010

Kempley has always been famous for its cider; indeed it was said that local folk were long lived because of drinking it. Perhaps this was so, for one Vicar, the Revd. Peter Senhouse, was in office for sixty-seven years, and Rudder's 1779 history noted that one household of sixteen persons had not known a death in living memory! The villagers are even more fortunate. Most areas have interesting churches to visit: this has two.

The red sand-stone church of St. Edward the Confessor, built in 1903 by the 7th Earl Beauchamp, should be visited first. It is a perfect example of the Arts and Crafts Movement, using local materials, stone from the Forest of Dean, timber such as that for the oak scissor-beams cut green from the Beauchamp estate, and local craftsmen. It has an unusual latticed-window known locally as the Jam Tart Window. The lectern and wooden candlesticks, in oak with mother-of-pearl inlay and ebony and holly stringing, were designed by Edward Barnsley and made by Ernest Gimson in the Daneway Workshops.

The primary reason for seeking out Kempley though is the small church of St. Mary, built seven hundred years earlier, between 1090 and 1100, possibly on the bridle-path between Hereford and Gloucester. Now some distance from the present village which gradually moved uphill to avoid floods and fog, it contains the most astonishing frescoes of c.1130–40, depicting St. Peter and the Apostles, "Our Lord in Majesty" with his feet resting on a globe, and the de Lacy family to whom William the Conqueror gave the manor. In its completeness the Kempley cycle is unique. To realise their importance one has only to remember that when Giotto (1266–1336) was in the midst of his great work these paintings were already 150 years old.

They were however nearly lost to us. White-washed over at the time of the Reformation, hidden for hundreds of years, not until 1872 did the Vicar, Revd. Arthur Drummond, rediscover signs of colour under the white-wash. Now we can marvel at these exquisite murals which began life as aids to help the village priest teach his illiterate flock the rudiments of the Christian faith.

MITCHELDEAN

ST. ANTHONY'S WELL

Location: One mile south of Mitcheldean, south of the A4136. Sheet 162 67081517

Lively wells or springs bringing fertility were regarded in heathen times as the dwelling place of powerful spirits to whom prayer and sacrifice were due, honoured with religious ceremonies, even decorated with flowers and green branches — and in some places this still happens. Certain of these wells became endowed with magical healing properties, and naturally this continued after the arrival of Christianity, though the Church would not allow them to be used for the performance of cures until they had been blessed by a Bishop and placed under the auspices of some saint.

Belief in the curative power of wells has persisted, quite apart from those 'medicinal springs' which became the centre-pieces of fashionable spas. Nothing seems able to eradicate this belief: how many of us will pass a 'wishing well' without throwing in, superstitiously, a coin or two?

Between the little villages of Flaxley and Gunsmills (named from the weapons cast there in the early part of the seventeenth century) at the confluence of four streams, a spring issues forth into a hollow. Here has been built in stone an exit for the water, a conduit and steps down into a bath. No matter what the weather, the water is a constant temperature — icy cold — and never fails to flow.

'Stow' names can suggest holy places that had wells respected as sacred long before the Saxons took control of England. *Merstow* indicates a sacred place on a boundary: This place was *Merstowe* before it was given its present name. Of deep pre-Christian religious significance, the well took its name not from a visit of some saint but from an itching skin disease which reached epidemic proportions in medieval times, and was called '*St. Anthony's Fire*'. People who bathed in the well were apparently cured by the icy cold water. Even earlier than that, the well was known for its curative powers. When the monks were at Flaxley Abbey they would send anyone suffering from a skin disease with instructions to bathe here on the first nine mornings in May.

Belief in the therapeutic power of this water continues to the present, but what complaints can now be cured? Probably more than by many branded remedies — if your faith is strong enough.

DRYBROOK

A COLD WIND AND A CAREFUL EMPLOYER

Location: Half-a-mile north of Drybrook, north of the A4136. Sheet 162 64421836

Drybrook has been called "probably the most consistently horrible village in the Forest" — but it has a most eccentric building.

Formerly the Euroclydon Hotel, somewhat uncommercially named after a cold, vindictive east wind, built on a hill above the village, it is now a residential home for elderly people, but still proclaims its name in large letters. It is a large black-and-white building, architecturally unremarkable except for a five-storey square tower erupting from the south side, adorned with a wrought-iron balcony looking north over the roof of the house.

Why was such a curious and out-of-place structure put up? Strangely, it was not for eccentric but for apparently sound reasons. A wealthy mine-owner, J.B. Bain, had it built in 1876 in order to provide a better vantage point from which to keep a watchful eye on his workers without leaving home, so the story goes; now it is used as a loft for the owner's doves.

RUARDEAN

FISHES FAR FROM WATER

Location: North of the A4136, fourteen miles west of Gloucester. Sheet 162 62101758

Set in the high part of the Forest (Ruardean Hill is the highest point) overlooking the beautiful Wye Valley, St. John the Baptist is one of a series of ancient churches on the forest fringe.

The somewhat lop-sided south porch has a thirteenth-century outer door with a sculptured head over it, probably that of the Blessed Virgin Mary. It is the inner door though that contains the tympanum representing St. George and the Dragon, remarkable both for its subject and for the quality of the carving: the mason must have been a man of great talent. Only three other tympana depicting St. George have survived in England. Does this suggest that the church's original dedication was to this saint? It has been suggested further, in view of the elevated position of the church, that the figure in the tympanum might be St. Michael. Fortunately it is in such good condition that there is no doubt the flowing sculpture depicts a furious St. George attacking a rather weedy Dragon, more like a large worm. But where did the mason get his inspiration? It appears that the model for St. George on horseback is taken from that at Parkenay-le-Vieux, where the subject is actually Constantine.

On a small stone plaque now set in the south wall of the nave is a carving of two fishes, almost certainly part of the original decoration of the doorway arch, but which got away 700 years ago. They were discovered in 1956 in the lining of the baking oven of a cottage at Turner's Tump, and identified as the product of the Herefordshire school of travelling craftsmen. It is thought they formed part of a frieze and were probably removed with builder's rubble when the south porch was built c.1200–50 — so other sections may yet be discovered and returned to their rightful place.

LITTLEDEAN

CRIME AND PUNISHMENT

Location: On the A4151, ten miles west of Gloucester. Sheet 162 67281362

The church is dedicated to St. Ethelbert who was murdered by his father-in-law, Offa, in the eighth century and over whose body Hereford Cathedral was built. The clock on the tower really is the most odd contraption, but this is compensated below in the churchyard which has an excellent collection of Forest of Dean headstones. Many have highly original designs characteristic of the area, and are expertly carved. But grief and sadness are recorded everywhere.

One head-stone records the local tragedy of four youths killed in a pit accident and another that of a policeman killed whilst apprehending poachers. Samuel Beard was thirty-seven years of age, and according to the inscription with its idiosyncratic spelling and use of uppercase letters:

Late a Police sergeant at Littledean
who was brutally beaten by four Men at the
Speech House when in the discharge of his duty
on the night of 17 August and died from
the effects on 24 August 1861.
Esteemed and Respected by the whole
Force for his Integrity Punctuality and
Exemplary discharge of his various duties
Oerwhelm'd with pain I Sink within This Cell
And bid the ancious cares of life farewell
Farewell Fond wife and you my Children dear
In whom was Centered All my Earthly Care.

What suffering lies behind the epitaph to John Bobin, who died on 4 October, 1871, aged only sixteen years, and again with local spelling and smattering of capital letters?

Long lingering sickness He endured
And many weary Months of pain
Kind tender friend did all She coall
To save his life but all in vain.

The House of Correction is one of Sir George Onesipherus Paul's four identical gaols built in the county in 1791, and the best preserved. Designed by the London architect, William Blackburn, great care was taken in the lay-out and in the detail of the fittings: in particular, the iron adjustable louvres, cell signalling-flaps, and centre-pivoted barred doors are remarkable for their appropriateness in maintaining security and their modernity.

The high walls conceal the inner buildings, from which only two inmates ever escaped — one broke his leg falling from the wall and was recaptured in a near-by pig-sty; the other crossed the Severn and was captured in Stroud. Sentenced for indecent assault and "uncomparable filthery", another prisoner was made to wear a dress in the hope that he would mend his ways. A keeper, matron, parson and teacher staffed the prison. In-mates had day and night cells and were allowed a leg of lamb and "fair" allocations of bread weekly. A treadmill tells of a less lenient regime.

AWRE

A MORTUARY CHEST

Location: East of the A48, ten miles south-west of Gloucester. Sheet 162 70900810

Tucked away in a loop of the Severn, Awre was an early settlement. It is described as *Alre* in a Saxon Cartulary of 832, and derives its name from the Old English *Alor*, meaning alder trees. A church here is one of the few actually referred to in the Domesday Book, when it contained twelve hides and was charged with the provision of "one ½ night's Ferm", ie required to pay as much produce as would provide for the maintenance of the Royal Court for a night. Clearly here was an important church and passage across the Severn.

The present church of St. Andrew has altered little since it was built in the early 1200s, except for the addition of the embattled Perpendicular west tower. In this tower, behind a modern glass screen, lies the dark, melancholy shape of an 800-year-old Mortuary Chest — a more impressive memorial to the Severn's victims than any fretted tombstone. Measuring eight feet long and three feet high, roughly cut from the trunk of one massive tree, the adze tool-marks plainly visible in its hollowed-out interior, this vast ancient chest, though possibly intended originally for vestments and books when at the Synod of 1290 every Parish was ordered to provide one, has been the temporary resting place for 'laying-out' many a drowned body recovered from the river.

This was obviously a frequent occurrence. The Parish Register records for 18 March, 1731:

> *This night about 10 the Newnham of Newnham, Trow, John Pierce, Owner, struck upon the Sand a little above Amity Crib and he and all the passengers to the number of 17 perished only 4 rowing in the small boat escaped.*

On the other hand, people buried here may not always *requiscat in pace* for in 1733 we read:

> *Buried Dec. 2nd. N.B. This body was stolen out of the grave the same night by Saml. Steele, Thos. Sallens, Rich Newman, Jas. Lane.*

Musically, St. Andrew's has a major claim to fame. The Parish Register dated 1579 reads:

> *Let it be remembered for the honour of this Parish that from it first sounded out the Psalms of David in English Metre.*

These metrical Psalms were the work of two local men, Thomas Sternhold and John Hopkins, and in the history of English church music were an important milestone.

Outside in the churchyard is a good collection of Forest head stones, the majority depicting the local speciality of multiple cherub heads — one with as many as eight — and show great skill in their execution combined with a charming naive symbolism in choice of subject, such as weeping willow trees and heavenly crowns. One stone has two cherub heads at the top, the twin on the right being awake with eyes open, the other on the left asleep with eyes closed. There is also a unique stone designed very much like a beehive. Carrying no inscription, but a carved top, it is squat and overlooked near the lych gate. Or is it a collapsed table-tomb merely piled in a corner? You will have to satisfy yourself about that.

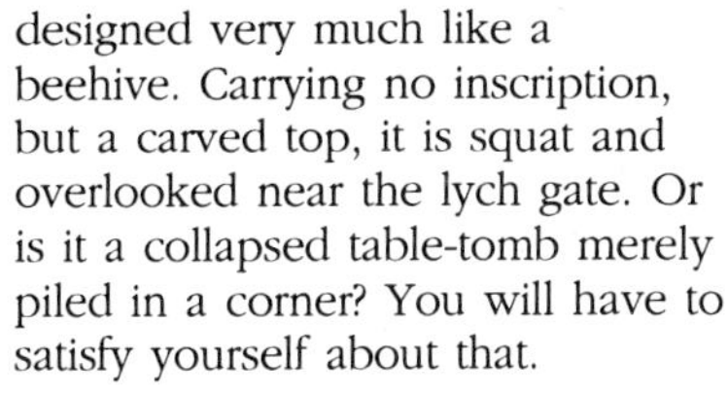

COLEFORD

A GOTHIC FOLLY

Location: South of A4136, sixteen miles south-west of Gloucester. Sheet 162 57501052

Coleford is a small, unremarkable place, neither beautiful nor ancient, and dominated by a large factory to the south, but contains what is probably the Forest's most unexpected pleasure.

Though no doubt the designer wished it to look like a miniature fortress, The Rock House in Newland Street is a nineteenth-century Gothick sham castle, now rendered and painted like a pink and white marshmallow, more at home in a seaside fairground than in an economically deprived area. It has no certain provenance. The architect may have been the Revd. Henry Poole, Vicar of Coleford from 1818, who was passionately fond of building and designed churches at Coleford, Parkend, Bream and Berry Hill.

To become a "Free-miner" a man has to be born within the Hundred of the Forest. The threatened closure of the maternity hospital here has raised the argument that this condition will be rendered impossible in the future: not only will "free-miners" become an endangered species, but their ancient, medieval rights will be eroded — something successive generations have jealously failed to achieve by other means.

It may be an unremarkable village and a "Free-house" has closed but it still stands proud and bears its unique name and logo of a globe for all to see: "Help Me Through The World". Who gave this name to a public house? Was life so grim and foreboding, so spirit-numbing and hopeless that the men of Coleford needed its services and its beverages before they could face the world outside its doors?

LYDNEY

AN UNUSUAL DEITY

Location: On the A48, eighteen miles south-west of Gloucester.	Sheet 162 61570265

Defensible positions on steep hill spurs close to the Severn have long been of strategic value, both for the control of trade routes along the river and for access to the riches of the estuary — fish, salt, reeds, and wildfowl.

One mile west of Lydney, on a wooded spur overlooking the Severn, at the end of the third century or early in the fourth, an elegant temple complex was built, including a guest house, baths and stalls dedicated to the worship of the god Nodens. The temple is unique in two ways: because of this deity who is otherwise unknown, and because its layout foreshadowed that of early Christian religious buildings in the following centuries and may have been built by followers of one of the early lost rivals to Christianity.

So just who was Nodens? This previously unknown god may have evolved from an early Celtic Irish or German god, 'Nodens the Catcher', with a magic hand, who survived in Irish legend as Nuadha (Argat-lam 'of the silver hand') and in Welsh legend as Lludd Llaw Ereint, the original King Lear. Both Nuadha and Lludd were involved in defending their kingdoms against invaders, the latter being the legendary king of Britain who fortified London and was buried at Ludgate. At London and Lydney he may have been a god of the headland guarding a great estuary and thus a notional tutelary god.

The location of the site on hilly ground overlooking the salmon runs of the Severn estuary suggest that his magic hand may have helped him as a divine fisherman. However, there is another, and not necessarily contradictory theory. Finds show that here was a god of healing, to whom pilgrims offered votive model figures of dogs, including a fine bronze greyhound and other cult objects. In classical religions dogs were widely associated with cults of healing. Sacred dogs were known in temples in Greece and Rome, and healed illnesses by licking the affected part of worshippers' bodies.

The patrons of Lydney were perhaps the wealthy Romanised Celts of great Cotswold villas such as Chedworth. Built in the closing years of the Roman empire, when Britain was already under threat of barbarian invasion and paganism was giving ground to Christianity, Lydney looks like an act of defiance against a new order.

TUTSHILL

IS IT REALLY A LOOK-OUT TOWER?

Location: One mile north of Chepstow, where A48 meets B4228. Sheet 162 53319468

Tutshill was a favoured residential village at the beginning of the nineteenth century. Communication with Bristol by water and an ideal situation overlooking the Wye gorge contributed to the number of fine houses and villas of this date. Eleven centuries earlier, Offa's dyke had been started about three-quarters of a mile away.

In between these dates, on top of a hill overlooking Chepstow castle and the river, had been built a look-out tower. It is now just a ruined shell of rubble and is listed only Grade III because no-one knows what it was, whether it was used as a prospect tower, or for military purposes. Or was it, as many locals think, a windmill? *Tut* as in Tutshill means watch-tower in the local dialect, so it may have had a military significance — but there is a fireplace, and would the builder have been so concerned about the comfort of a mere sentry?

Though views differ, no-one falls out about it. Perhaps that is why the local pub is called, uniquely, 'Live And Let Live'.

Along the road to Parson's Allotment in Tidenham Chase, a tall standing stone was raised not for any druidical purpose but to commemorate Queen Victoria's Jubilee.

STAUNTON

ROCKS AND STONES

Location: Off the A4136, on the outskirts of Staunton. Sheet 162 54601242

High on the Forest rim between Staunton and the Wye, looking down over the oaks, rowan and silver birch, stands a huge mottled form of stone. The Buckstone is an ancient phenomenon, jutting over the road and resembling some prehistoric monster. Once, this great grey mass 'bucked' or rocked on its narrow base, but no more for this symbol of the mysterious past of Dean is held together by concrete, and a huge pin holds it firmly to its pedestal. It was broken in 1885 when a group of exuberant, inebriated visitors rolled it down the hill. It took many horses to pull it back again, to be fixed permanently to its base. But the magic remains and legends still drift around this massive stone and its age-old partners the Near Hearkening and the Far Hearkening Stones down-hill among the trees. For tradition holds that the sound of the rocking stone carried through the earth to listening stones down the hill, and so messages could pass through them and across the Wye and into the heart of Wales. Legends tell us that this was a place for Druid sacrifices and for beheading criminals. Nearby is a hollow rock, but was it really shaped for a victim's head and a channel for the blood, or is this just a freak of geology? There is a similar hollowed stone at the Toad's Mouth below, another great rock near the Staunton-Monmouth road.

A legend in verse explains how the Buckstone got its name. It tells of the young Druid bard, Teudor, standing near the stone one evening at sunset, sadly surveying the forests which were being infiltrated by Roman advance parties, when a silent procession of Druid priests approached, having been commanded to sacrifice the first living thing they saw. As they sadly prepared to sacrifice the young Teudor, a buck, closely pursued by a wolf, leapt onto the stone and lay there exhausted by its headlong flight while the wolf slunk off deprived of its prey.

By the Near Hearkening Stone is the Suck Stone. Lozenge-shaped, and again of local conglomerate, it is by far the largest detached rock in the Forest and most probably in England, estimated to contain some 14,000 tons. Long ago it fell from the rock above, but may have got its name from being the meeting place of some old *soccage* court. The Long Stone stands beside the road from Coleford to Staunton (ref 55941220). It is called 'the bleeding stone', because if at midnight a pin is stuck into the grey mass it will bleed and then drag itself groaning down through the woods to the river.

NEWLAND

MEDIEVAL FORESTERS AND MINERS

Location: One-and-a-half miles south of Coleford, south of A4136. Sheet 162 55310958

The Free Miners of the Forest are proud and protective of their status, which came about several hundred years ago. During the siege of Berwick-on-Tweed in the twelfth century, King John called for Forest of Dean miners to help in tunnelling a passage so the army could storm the castle: in this way the siege was accomplished successfully. In return the King gave the miners a charter, for *tyme out of mynd*, to mine for coal anywhere in the Forest of Dean and that from then henceforth they would be known as *Free Miners.*

Consequently, all the mineral rights belong to the Free Miners, and they must be granted a licence to work anywhere in the Forest. There are though certain qualifications: they must have worked in a coal mine already for at least a year and a day, and they must have been born within the Hundred of St. Briavels.

Newland — the origin of the name is obvious — began like many Forest villages as a new clearing in a valley. Its church of All Saints is often called 'The Cathedral of the Forest' — and indeed advertises itself as such on the bill-board outside — because of its wide aisles and splendid proportions. It has, also, the richest collection of early effigies in the district, some of which are unique, and throw light on the early Free Miners and others connected with the Forest.

The font is mid-fifteenth century, and though of rather crude local workmanship, the Miners are included in a position of equality with aristocratic landowners. The chamfer has eight heater-shaped shields bearing the devices of the Free Miners and the Free Smiths of the Forest, as well as more noble arms of Buckingham, Warwick and Serjaunt.

To the west of the font lies the unique effigy of the Forester of Fee, showing interesting details of the hunting costume of the mid-fifteenth century. On his right hangs his hunting horn and on his left his sword and knife. His cap is drawn back in plaits and tied. There is an inscription in English, giving his name Wrall, Forester of Fee, (Jenkin Wyrall)

> . . . *which dysesyd on the VIII day of Synt Lauroc*
> *the yeare of oure Lorde MCCCCLVII.*

In comparison, at the east end of the south aisle lies a flat slab with the incised figure of a bowman, complete with bow, horn, dagger and large-brimmed hat; he is early seventeenth century.

In the south chancel chapel are the brasses of c.1445 to Robert Gryndour and his wife. The husband's brass depicts him in armour, but his head is bare, showing a luxuriant beard; another rare feature is the pauldron used in tilting instead of a shield. The words *Sir Christopher Baynham Knt* have been incised on the slab between the figures, but this was in 1557, a century after their deaths, when some-one got mixed up.

On this slab is a separate brass plate of later insertion but unknown origin, which is generally considered the most curious. It is a helmet, mantling and crest which depicts a medieval miner of the Forest with hod and pick (his *maddock* or *mattock*) in hand and a candlestick (his *nelly*) in his mouth. It is one foot in length and is unique not only for its subject, but also for its technique, as the figure is shown in relief.

A strangely incongruous note is struck by the sign outside the thirteenth-century inn which looks down over the churchyard. A huge and ugly bird displays its bony legs and feathered rump outside the Ostrich, an inn which might have been expected to display the arms of the lords or knights whose tabletombs adorn the church, or something related to the coaching trade. Perhaps, however, *The Ostrich* is appropriate to a village which kept its head firmly in the sand while the Industrial Revolution whirled round the Forest, devastating many a village as it passed — but not this one.

ST. BRIAVELS

UPSTAIRS, DOWNSTAIRS

Location: Five miles south of Coleford. Sheet 162 55880465

St. Briavels was once the administrative centre of the Forest of Dean, giving its name to the Hundred upon which the Forest is based, and the castle, built during the reign of Henry I, the headquarters of the King's presence, declared boldly by the Hunter's Horn badge of the Constable of the Forest on a unique, elaborately-carved, gabled and spired chimney stack — impossible to miss or mistake.

Our forefathers travelled to St. Briavels to pick a quarrel, for the village was famous for them: Henry III alone used 6,000 in the year 1223. They were the quarrels, or arrow-heads, fired from crossbows, and though they have long since disappeared, the Tump on the village green is formed from the cinders of the fires in which they were forged.

St. Briavel's water and Whyrals wheat
Are the best bread and water King John ever eat.

There is a vague tradition that King John was a prisoner within the castle: certainly there is a room designated 'the prison' with the coupley inscribed on the wall.

This though is no ordinary prison cell, for it contains a large fireplace and a garde robe — all medieval mod cons, in fact. Nor were the prisoners incarcerated mere ordinary people. For example, inscribed on the prison wall are drawings of three windmills and a treasure chest. Although there are no windmills in the area there are three wells in the village and the graffiti has been interpreted as confirming the existence of buried treasure, rumoured to be silver coins from the Civil War period.

Who was the author of a message scratched onto the prison wall, and who was the Robin Belcher it refers to? Despite some idiosyncratic spelling and orthography, the writer was clearly no ordinary forester, as he was literate in an age when this was rare. What length of sentence had he served in prison, and had Robin Belcher given false evidence against him?

ROBIN BELCHER THE DAY
WILL COM THAT THOU SHALL
AN SWER FOR IT FOR
THOU HAST SWORN
AGAINEST ME 1674
MY DIAS IS ROON
IT. TIS T TIME I WAS
GONE FOR I HAVE
BIN AGRET SPA
CE AND I AM WEARY
OF THE PLA CE

Roon is local dialect for 'running out'.

For those not kept in the upstairs prison, a form of execution administered in the castle was *oubliette*, which means 'to forget'. The prisoner was thrown into a twenty-four-foot shaft, which can still be seen in the dungeon beneath the gatehouse, the trap door was closed and, if he did not die from the fall, he did of starvation.

Facing the castle gatehouse is the church of St. Mary the Virgin. The site has been a place of worship since the Celts, but it was the Normans who built the first stone church here, c.1086. There are curiosities to be explored. In the Lady Chapel is an Easter Tomb with a decorated slab of Forest stone, made for the tomb of Robert, Abbot of Lire, in France, who died in St. Briavels in 1272. But a woman's head has been superimposed, in different stone and of unknown identity. So who is she and does she now lie with Abbot Robert? Is he happy about that?

There is also a most interesting late sixteenth-century tomb with complete semi-reclining effigies of William Warren and his wife, who appear to be taking their present state in a quite leisurely manner. Their four children at prayer below are much more in keeping with the style of the time.

The Norman font, though not outstanding itself, stands on a frill of sixteen lobes, projecting horizontally, which is quite unique. The projections are hardly decorative, so what long-forgotten purpose did they serve?

ENGLISH BICKNOR

A HEART BURIAL?

Location: North of the A4136, three miles north of Coleford. Sheet 162 58211577

There are not many villages whose names are prefixed by the country of their origin to distinguish them from another across the border. This name may have been derived from *Bica's Ridge* with *Bica* a Saxon lord of the Manor; or the name *Bicknor* or *Bicanofre* may mean 'over or above the river'. Whichever, 'English' is used to differentiate it from 'Welsh' Bicknor on the other side of the Wye.

Built within fifty years of the Norman Conquest, and therefore older than the famous ruins of Tintern Abbey further down the valley, the site of St. Mary the Virgin's church was already of great antiquity, partly surrounded by Offa's Dyke which was the frontier between England and Wales, in an oval churchyard of Saxon origin, and in the outer courtyard of a motte and bailey, one of the many such earthworks on the Welsh border. This one may date from the reign of King Stephen and was destroyed in the mid-thirteenth century; the castle moat still surrounds the churchyard.

From outside, the church offers no expectation of the splendid Norman work within. However, it is one of the monuments which the visitor will find puzzling.

Though not of high quality, and characteristic of the period, their long gowns caught up under their arms, two female effigies of c.1300 and 1350 are thought to be 'the true patron' of the church, Lady Cecilia de Muchegros, her feet on a dog, and her great grand-daughter Lady Harwisia de Bures, who died before 1348. The latter is depicted holding an object thought to be a heart. If this is so, it would signify a heart burial, the body being interred elsewhere, and the only one in this part of the county. Or is it an egg she is carrying, which was the ancient symbol of the Resurrection (NB Easter Eggs)? If this latter explanation is correct, the symbol is most unusual, only two others being known. Look carefully, and make up your own mind.

There is yet another puzzle here. The capitals of the Norman pillars which dominate the interior are decorated with rich sculpture, each designed differently with scallops and broad leaves ending in volutes.

At the eastern end of the north arcade is what surely must have been the arch of a doorway: but a doorway to where? Was this the original south doorway? Its sculpture, with rich chevrons, is of even higher quality than on the capitals. The carvings of beak-heads are especially fine and spirited, one with its tongue poking out at you, one eating a duck, its neck and head not yet engorged but still hanging out of the monster's mouth. Nothing like this archway of three orders is found anywhere else in the district. Just who was this exceptionally talented mason, and who engaged him to carry out this work of such quality?

In the churchyard are several intriguing tombstones. Why did a young married girl die at the age of fourteen in 1706? Could it have been in childbirth or from some epidemic illness such as measles? What is the sad story behind the two young sisters who died of typhoid, the elder travelling to Australia to marry her sweetheart and buried at sea, the younger whose grave is here? How grievous was the heartache of a mother who buried five children all under the age of three years? What lies behind the simple inscription on another —

Charles, a black servant.

Was he a boy plucked from the hot climes of his native land and laid to rest in a Christian plot in a beautiful part of Gloucestershire?

SPEECH HOUSE

THE SCULPTURE TRAIL

Location: Off the B4226, thirteen miles south-west of Gloucester. Sheet 162 61601230

For those explorers prepared to leave the main roads, there are several trails through the Forest. One is quite unique, following a collection of original sculptures located within the woodland, the artists taking their inspiration from the forest setting, wildlife and history of the Dean.

You will never see them the same twice. The passing seasons, the constantly changing light through the trees, present new perspectives from moment to moment on these works of art. This is an innovative way of exploring the forest, with the exhibits providing new delights at each turn along the meandering route.

At the roadside is an unprepossessing pillar marking the traditional centre of the Forest. It was raised by Viscount Bledisloe to mark the fiftieth year of his service as a Verderer, an office instituted by Cnut in the early eleventh century and charged with the duty of guarding of the vert and the venison on behalf of the King.

BIBLIOGRAPHY

Odd and Unusual England, John Bland. Spurbooks

The Gloucestershire Village Book, Federation of W.I.

The Secret Forest of Dean, Fay Godwin. Arnolfini

The Shell Book of English Villages, John Hadfield. Michael Joseph

Follies, Gwyn Headley and Wim Meulenkamp. Jonathan Cape

Follies and Grottos, Barbara Jones.

The Victoria History of the County. Oxford University Press

County Curiosities of England, Lynn Parr. This England.

Tales of Old Gloucestershire, Betty Smith. Countryside Books

Timpson's Towns, John Timpson. Jarrold

Gloucestershire Vol 2, David Verey. Penguin

The Archaeology and History of Ancient Dean, Bryan Walters. Thornhill Press

The Deerhurst Angel, Priory Church of St. Mary, Deerhurst

THE AUTHORS

This is the second collaborative publication by the authors. Totalled together, they have lived for more than six decades in the area, worked in it and travelled through it daily, yet retained their ardent, undimmed fascination for its history and culture. Thus they bring to this book their own unique synthesis of the curiosities, oddities and eccentricities not seen by the visitor concerned to encompass a total perspective of the area — indeed not known even by many who live here — but who, as with the authors, will not fail to be amazed by its very richness and variety. In their professional lives both authors worked intensively with individual people, so they have taken particular interest not only in the curiosities and artefacts per se but in the people who created them, the purposes they were meant to serve, and how they acquired explanatory myths.

Waterwheel, Hartpury Mill

INDEX

Art From Old Scrap, Hasfield Court